MW00588135

CARIBBEAN WRITERS SERIES

32

Jestina's Calypso

CARIBBEAN WRITERS SERIES

Jestina's Calypso
& other plays

EARL LOVELACE

HEINEMANN
LONDON · KINGSTON · PORT OF SPAIN

Heinemann Educational Books Ltd
22 Bedford Square, London WC1B 3HH
PO Box 1028, Kingston, Jamaica
27 Belmont Circular Road, Port of Spain, Trinidad

IBADAN NAIROBI
EDINBURGH MELBOURNE AUCKLAND
SINGAPORE HONG KONG KUALA LUMPUR NEW DELHI

© Earl Lovelace 1984
First published 1984

British Library Cataloguing in Publication Data

Lovelace, Earl
    Jestina's calypso and other plays. – Caribbean
    writers series; v.32)
    I. Title   II. Series
    812   PR6062.085

    ISBN 0-435-98751-8

Set in 10/11 Baskerville by
Performance Typesetting Ltd, Milton Keynes
Printed in Great Britain by Richard Clay,
(The Chaucer Press) Ltd, Bungay, Suffolk

For
Walt, Che and Lulu

Contents

Jestina's Calypso

Play in Two Acts

Dedicated to Aldwyn Boynes

Jestina's Calypso was first performed by the UWI players on 17, 18 and 23 March 1978 with the following cast:

JESTINA, Wendy Diaz/Hazel Thompson
LAURA, Sandra Bushell
PRETTYPIG, Joan Osbourne
MAKO, Allyson Stephens
PAPPYSHOW, Rooney Beckles
TOTO, Rawle Harriot
DOCTOR, Anthony Bramble
Directed by Gregory McGuire

Characters

JESTINA, woman of 39. Owner of a little struggling parlour
LAURA, woman of 32, but looks 26. Hairdresser/Seamstress
PRETTYPIG, ex-jamettee, now water-carrier on road project
MAKO, busybody housewife
PAPPYSHOW, whe-whe mark carrier
TOTO, lottery vendor and macho-man
DOCTOR, road worker near retirement

Act One

Scene One

SET: *The stage is divided into two: one side a level higher than the next. Left is the street corner. Right is* JESTINA *'s house cum parlour.* TOTO *wears cast-off police clothing: boots and a bus conductor's cap throughout.*
DOCTOR *has his lottery set up on a push cart.*
JESTINA *'s place is in darkness. As lights go up,* MAKO, PAPPYSHOW *and others are singing:*

> January come, she nuh married
> February come, she nuh married
> March coming and she nuh married
> she nuh go married again
>
> April come she nuh married
> May come she nuh married
> June coming and she nuh married
> she nuh go married again
>
> July come she nuh married
> August come she nuh married
> September coming and she nuh married
> she nuh go married again
>
> October come she nuh married
> November come she nuh married
> December coming and she nuh married
> She nuh go married again
> She nuh go married again.

PAPPYSHOW [*hailing*]: Aye! Jestina! The car coming! Come out! Come out, Queen of Ugliness.
PRETTYPIG: Shhh! Not so loud [*nudging* MAKO]. He always so loud and scandalous, like he alone have mouth.

MAKO: What you shhhing him for? Ain't everybody know
already that is today the man coming. It ain't have no
secret in this place.

PAPPYSHOW [*maliciously, amused*]: I want to know what that fella
would do when he see that woman face; that is what I
want to know. Toto, [*turning and addressing* TOTO] boy, what
would you do if you had a pen pal who you write to, and
you come all this distance, this five thousand or how much
miles it is, from away, on one of them big jet aeroplanes
that does tremble the whole island when they land, come
with gladness beating in your heart, like them Texaco
machines pumping oil out of the earth chest . . . You come
to meet this pen pal, this craft to spend a time with her, a
holiday —

MAKO [*with certainty*]: Is not holiday he coming on, you know. Is
married the man coming to married.

PRETTYPIG [*astonished*]: Married?

TOTO: Married? With ring and veil and thing? She? [*looks to*
MAKO, *questioning.* MAKO *nods*] What the arse does wrong
with people, boy?

DOCTOR [*grunting in an almost moaning way*]: Hummm!
Hummm!

PAPPYSHOW: I mean, what would you do, boy? If a woman with
Jestina face come and meet you in the airport and say
she's your pen pal? What would you do Toto?

PRETTYPIG [*thoughtful, reflecting but somewhat mocking*]: But if . . . if
married involve, this is serious business. Is serious
business. [*with surprise*] Jestina serious!

PAPPYSHOW [*hailing, teasing, loud*]: Jestina! Bring that face out
here, girl. Bring it. [*he begins to clap hands and sing*] Bring it,
bring it.

The others join in (DOCTOR *alone is subdued).*

Bring it with a willing mind
The Lord said to you
Be generous and True
Bring it with a willing mind

Girl bring it, bring it
Bring it with a willing mind
I say to you
Be generous and true
Bring it with a willing mind

PAPPYSHOW [*leading the chant*]:
Bring the face
I say, bring the face
I want the face
I want the face
The pretty face
The nice face
The bold face
The old face
The cold face.

TOTO [*laughing a heartfelt laughter to himself, his tone reflective*]:
What I would do, boy? What I would do if this woman . . .
if this thing happen to me, eh? What I would do?

PAPPYSHOW: And when you come through the Customs gate in
your latest wear, spitting Yankee, she step up to you in
front all them people who coming from New York too,
with camera round their neck and tie and jacket and fancy
dress . . .

TOTO [*chuckling*]: Bermuda shorts!

PRETTYPIG: But you know, this Jestina really brave in truth.

PAPPYSHOW: In front tourists with Bermuda shorts and natives
waiting with gladiolis and hibiscus and anthuriums and
roses. In front people with roses, Toto . . .

MAKO [*mischievously*]: But if the man like she?

PAPPYSHOW: And she hug you up and buss a big kiss on your
mouth. Pax! in front of everybody? What would you do
Toto? As man, what would you do?

PRETTYPIG [*more serious and concerned*]: No. But imagine, in truth
that a woman with Jestina face could have so much guts,
could be so brave, so . . .

DOCTOR [*as if he had been thinking about it all the time*]:
Courageous.

TOTO [*triumphantly. He has it now*]: You know what I would do?

PRETTYPIG: Courageous and bold and wicked to her own self to
write this man . . .

DOCTOR: People does be born so. People does be born with that
courage and guts and wickedness in them [*he pauses
heavily*].

TOTO: You know what I would do . . .

PRETTYPIG: To write this man far off where he is in England or
America [*looking at* MAKO *for verification*] and tell him she
loves him. Love? [PAPPYSHOW *smiles*] No. You all laughing.
You could imagine the bravery Jestina must have in her
heart to go in the Post Office and post this letter inviting
the man to come here, and the wicked faith to believe that
after he see her face . . . that face . . .

DOCTOR: People does born with a kinda tall craziness in their
blood, like a hunting dog, that does make them fling
themself against a wild beast world ten times stronger and
faster and more cunning. They does born with a kinda
ferocious stupidity that is more than guts. Is more than
courage, is a . . . is . . . is a beast-animal wickedness. [*he
speaks tremblly, haltingly, trying to hurry, but not really hurrying,
for he expects to be interrupted. But for once they listen*] Campo
have a small little pot hound dog big so [*measuring with his
hands*], that will attack a lion. You know it [*looking at*
TOTO]. The big eye black and white one. Is a kinda mad
wicked strength and belief they have inside them. Little
Man, the stickfighter, had it. He would go in the ring
against the best stickman, and by a kinda stubbornness, a
kinda wicked persistent coming in, coming in . . .

PAPPYSHOW [*to blunt* DOCTOR*'s spell*]: Little man? So much stick
buss open his head, was a shame to see him. Fellars don't
want to play him, but still a drum can't beat if he ain't
jumping in the ring.

DOCTOR: You had to beat him, beat him, beat him. You had to
buss open his head in truth, and close down his two eye to
stop him. Cause he there coming in, grinning. And all the

blows you hit him still can't drive him back.

TOTO: One carnival I see him play a wood against Merry, the
King. Merry make him a wood: Wap! Straight down
across his temple, and Little Man fall down on his back,
and everybody saying, everybody shouting: Oh God, he
dead! Today he dead! And from right where he is there on
his back, as he going down, Little Man send back one
serious repeater, like a mappirire, right inside here
[*showing*] where Merry handjoin his shoulders, slide right
off Merry stick, break Merry jaw, yes. Break Merry jaw.
And when Merry jaw finish break, we just see blood self
dripping down Little Man face from the cut he get on his
temple. Then he fall down flat.

DOCTOR: I know good good stickman refuse to karay with him.
Them is dangerous people. You does have to kill them to
stop them. And one day they kill him. Fifteen of them
corner him by the market . . . You was there, Toto. Just
before it happen Gladys, Dustan wife, did bite off one of
Dustan ears . . . Fifteen of them. And he wouldn't run. He
fight them. He would't run. And after they get him on the
ground, they still keep beating him long after he stop
moving, they ain't know he dead, so fraid they was of him.
[*all grow serious*] That is why I say, you can't be more
wicked than the world.

PAPPYSHOW [*laughs*]: If you think she wicked, what about the
fella who coming for this wedding? What about him?

Throughout, TOTO *likes* PRETTYPIG *but is afraid to show it.*
PAPPYSHOW *likes* MAKO *but suffers a similar fear. They touch, etc. But
are afraid to reveal vulnerability.*

TOTO: If was me . . .

PRETTYPIG: What woman would want you? What you have to
offer, Toto?

TOTO *looks at her suggestively, grabs the front of his crotch.*

PRETTYPIG: That is all you have in your head.
TOTO: Not in my head. [*laughs*]

PRETTYPIG *looks at him stumped for an answer.*

TOTO: You know what I would do? I would faint away. I would
    just ups and faint away. Say is the heat. I can't stand the
    heat. Ask them to put me back on the plane. And is gone I
    gone. Home! I going back home.
MAKO: What home? The man from right here in this island.
    This here is home.
PRETTYPIG: You mean . . . you mean, his family will be there at
    the airport to meet him too. [*sorrowful pause*] Oh, Lord, no!
MAKO: He ain't have no family. Since he small so [*showing*] he
    leave and go away to the whiteman land. He grew up over
    there. I think he have citizenship too: that green card that
    Dolly daughter with the BA have.
PRETTYPIG [*outraged*]: And he coming back here?
DOCTOR: Here? He coming back here?
PRETTYPIG: What it have in this island to come back to? What?
    No. Serious. I mean, if I go away, if God help me and I
    manage to get out of this spit spot of an island, what I
    coming back here for? What could bring me back here?
    [*they look at her amazed*] True [*with sincerity*].
PAPPYSHOW: This is home. We have sunshine here.
PRETTYPIG: I going to have winter coat.
TOTO: Beaches with white sand.
PRETTYPIG: Swimming pool.
MAKO: We have democracee. Republic.
PRETTYPIG: Don't talk no politics to me at all at all, at all. I vote
    for William in sixty-one, and not a bitch getting me to
    stain my finger for him again.
DOCTOR [*languidly and with provoking certainty*]: You will come
    back for carnival.

They all smile and look at her triumphantly.

ALL: Yes, she will come back for carnival.

PRETTYPIG [*thoughtful and serious*]: You know, I wouldn't even
    come back for carnival.

TOTO [*accusing and outraged*]: You wouldn't come back for
    carnival? All Stars Steelband going down Charlotte Street,
    J'Ouvert morning . . .

MAKO: Panorama in the Savannah, the Queen Show, playing
    history in Saldenah band.

TOTO: A bottle ah rum in your back pocket, your cape over
    your shoulder, and a sword in your hand, and you
    chipping down the open road for everybody to see you
    holding up your man.

Group imitates a carnival brass band with trombones, bugles as they
syncopate. Sound: the wailing of brass bugles, carnival music,
syncopation of brassband music: dar dar! dar dar! dar! dar dar!

TOTO: You wouldn't come back for carnival?

MAKO: For all them fete for carnival? To hear Sparrow and
    Kitchener sing, and see Rose do she thing? You wouldn't
    come back for carnival?

PAPPYSHOW: You wouldn't come back for carnival? People like
    peas grain floating down the road and man and woman
    wining back and iron ringing, and pan pan pan. And to
    hear robber speech and watch jab jab whips crack across
    jab jab back, and sailors fulla rum tumble down in the
    gutter and get up back and let tourist snap your picture
    and your face full up with powder that See Bees throw.
    You wouldn't come back for that? You wouldn't come
    back?

MAKO: You wouldn't come back?

TOTO: You wouldn't come back?

DOCTOR: You wouldn't come back?

All eyes accuse her. PRETTYPIG'S *posture slackens in the face of their*
accusation and threat.

PRETTYPIG: Okay, Okay! I will come back for carnival.

They all hug her and they do a dance as they sing:

> Yes, she go come back for carnival
> yes, she go join in the bacchanal.

They all laugh with merriment.

TOTO [*on the sly, trying to pinch* PRETTYPIG]: This is a nice place
  girl.
MAKO: This place sweet!
PAPPYSHOW: Where else you could get bacchanal like this? A
  woman with Jestina face, with Jestina courage? [*he turns at
  the sound of an approaching car. The horn blows*]
MAKO [*excitedly*]: Look it! Look it! The car reach to take she to
  the airport.
ALL: It reach, it reach! It reach! [*they turn to* JESTINA*'s house*]
PAPPYSHOW: Jestina, girl, bring that face out here [*as an order*].

*All begin to sing: 'Bring it with a willing mind'. They jazz it up, dance
and shake like Shouters. They scream and laugh.* DOCTOR *reluctantly
takes something of a part.* MAKO *looks as if she wants to leave.*

PRETTYPIG: Where you going? Bacchanal now start.
MAKO [*excitedly*]: Oh, gosh! I have to go and get a taxi. I have to
  be there at the airport to see the man face when they meet.
PAPPYSHOW: You have time. Jestina putting on a new face.
  Jestina! [*hailing*]
TOTO: But . . . but . . . but suppose he is a monster just like she.
  Suppose he ain't no better looking. Not because he went
  away he bound to be good looking you know.
PRETTYPIG [*taking objection*]: What you say?
TOTO: I say, supposing he ugly too, he ain't bound to be a
  movie star. Dracula from America too.
PRETTYPIG [*authoritative*]: You ever see anybody ugly from
  away? Millicent had a daughter went to America with her
  mouth long so [*indicating*]. I see the girl when she went
  away, and I see she when she come back. I had was to ask:
  That is Barbara? That is Barbara? If you see how nice

Barbara get. The girl skin come smooth, smooth. Her nose was broad like the Gran Bocas, it get so straight . . . and with a little kinda round point. And if you hear her voice how it come . . . soft and light, soft and light, and refine. Like olive oil.

MAKO [*authoritative*]: Is the cold, you know. The winter that does refine you so. You remember Roland, Mr Carmichael son. I hear him when he come back from England speak from behind a curtain, I coulda swear was a whiteman. They say in the winter the refining does work better. It so cold if you go to talk your mouth can't open big. You can't say: Aaah [*opening her mouth broad*]. You have to say Oh [*delicately parting her lips*] and the cold breeze inside your nose too . . . it does make you talk proper.

TOTO: Maybe he could carry Jestina away and get her refine too.

PAPPYSHOW: Winter too mild to refine Jestina . . . Like she putting on a new face in truth. Jestina! [*loud*] JESTINA! Bring the blasted face and come here, girl.

TOTO [*singing*]:
> Oh what a disgrace
> When I look at Jestina face
> Water in my eye
> Woman you make me cry
> She must be mad
> To believe that in Trinidad
> A woman like she
> Could wrangle matrimony.

All join in chorus [*beating makeshift instruments*].

> Jestina, girl, who go married to you
> Jestina, girl, who go married to you
> Jestina, girl, who go married to you
> Cause your face like a whale
> Like you just come from jail!

They chant [*uproariously*].

> Bring your face
> I want the face
> The bad face
> The hard face
> The old face
> The bold face.

They laugh.

Scene Two

Lights up on JESTINA*'s bedroom.* JESTINA *is in half slip in front mirror, trying out one pose after another. She isn't satisfied. She's nervous, uneasy. She can't get her wig to stay properly. Outside, the song rises: 'Bring it, bring it with a willing mind'.*

JESTINA: I should have write and say I is a ugly woman, I not young any more; I live thirty-nine years in this narrow prison of an island, moving across its villages, weeding and toting water and cutlassing like a man, trying with my own hands to make a living and seeking to live, walking out of step with these giggling people whose one ambition is surviving. They don't even dream dreams here far more live them. Yes, I shoulda write and expose my whole self to him. Everything . . . And I is a lonely lonely woman who start out with nothing, with no inheritance of money or position in society, or special love from family; and I have too many dreams and I does hope too much, and I try too hard with people . . . I try too hard with people who don't know what a person is.

Outside: the song is jazzed up.

JESTINA [*reproachfully*]: And they batter me, they batter me well.
  Look me! My face was never my fortune, my body like a
  whip now [*patting her bottom*] and veins stand out on my
  hands like lianes in a old forest, and my face: wrinkles
  crawling cross it like wood ants tunnels inside a wood
  house that stand up too long. Look me! [*facing audience*]
  Twist up and mark up by time and lovers who never loved
  me, who never knew me . . . They never knew me. [*song
  outside rises: whistles blowing, tins beating. Reproaching self,
  softness*] I been too young, too innocent for too long, too
  ready to go again, too hurry to start up like a blasted old
  engine, to turn my ear to any voice that sound like it have a
  song. [*softening*] Is this thing in me, you know, this hope,
  this dream that will not let me go. And you know, it does
  pain afterwards, the time I waste on men who leave me as
  soon as they finish roll off my belly. [*tone of exasperation,
  vexed with self, stamping*] And still still I does come back
  again to bend like a blasted bamboo in another wind. [*she
  takes up her dress off the bed where it has been laid out. For a
  moment she grows affirming. The music is offensive and she
  addresses it defiantly*]. But I ain't break down yet. I here, you
  hear me. I here. And though I ain't have too much figure,
  my body still strong. I could go again. I know how to
  please a man. And I learn the one thing they teach in this
  island: manners. I have manners. I wouldn't embarrass
  you in front your friends. I would stay inside I would cook
  your food. I would know my place. You wouldn't turn me
  away?

The song comes up. JESTINA *puts on her dress. The singing stops. She
feels the silence. She is alone. She sits cautiously at the mirror. The wig is
not sitting properly. The car horn blows. She jumps, startled.
Immediately the crowd outside begin vociferous and derisive chant:*

The car come, she going now! The car come she going now!
The car come she going now!

PAPPYSHOW *and* TOTO *throw themselves down, make flips, roll.*
PRETTYPIG *and* MAKO *will try hypocritically to restrain them a little,
but they join in.* DOCTOR *smiles, with not so much embarrassment as
resignation.*

PAPPYSHOW : Give me her crown [*to* TOTO].

TOTO *folds a piece of branch into a circle and hands it to* PAPPYSHOW .
He dances around holding it up as the singing continues.

JESTINA [*trying to straighten the wig before the mirror*]: You wouldn't
turn me away. Is a winter here in this hot island. I here in
this sweating heat freezing for life, for your hand to warm
my own, for your eyes to see things with, to laugh with.
You think I too brave, too bold to want to live [*as if
suffocating*]. Here how they laugh me! Mad woman Jestina
is the name they give me. You understand? Mad. Mad. To
want to live, to want to be, to be a whole person, somebody
with a journey in front of me. [*she looks at herself in the mirror*]
No. I can't go to him. I can't go. I can't go. [*she sweeps a
hand across the dressing table, scattering the things. She throws
herself on the bed.*]

Outside: LAURA *crosses in front the crowd. They stop singing.*
PAPPYSHOW *has the crown in his hand.*

PAPPYSHOW : You going to visit the queen. Eh?

They sing in slow tempo:

> She is going to visit the queen
> She is going to visit the queen
> She is going up there with her curly hair
> She is going to visit the queen.

PAPPYSHOW [*shouting*]: Queen Jestina! I have your crown!

LAURA *knocks on the door. All laugh.*

[*Note: During this scene the crowds outside would carry on their jeering and scandalous behaviour. It begins with* PAPPYSHOW *as the main instigator of this mood, but as it continues, one by one, the others will be drawn more and more into the jeering until they all are part of it.*]

LAURA *knocks once. No answer. She pushes the door half cautiously.*
LAURA *five or six years younger, pretty in a smooth, superficial way.*

LAURA [*testingly*]: Jestina? [*she goes over to the bed where* JESTINA *is lying. Cautiously, puzzled*] What happen? You ain't ready yet? Girl, you don't know the car outside waiting? [*she looks around, takes in the condition of the dressing table, etc.*] What? [*indicating the mess. She takes things off the floor, begins to rearrange them.*] You not sick? Come [*with greater firmness*]. Let's get ready. Let's go.

JESTINA [*regretfully*]: Maybe yeas ago. Years ago, my skin at least was smooth and my body firm and I could move, and men didn't have to look at my face.

LAURA: Is just a little nervousness. I woulda be nervous too. Anybody would be nervous. Look [*taking up the wig*]. Put on the wig. Let me help you.

JESTINA *sits still as* LAURA *fixes the wig on her head.* LAURA *talks soothingly.*

LAURA: You worrying with those people. He coming today and you going to worry with those people. Come. How the wig looking now?

JESTINA [*anguished*]: I look just like a blasted masquerade. [*she tears off the wig and flings it from her*].

LAURA [*fetching the wig*]: Jestina, this is the day you waiting for for the last three months, for the last three years. You going to throw it away just because a mirror in front your face. Come, you better let me make you up again.

JESTINA [*weakening*]: Make up? Make up can't make me up.

The car horn blows outside.

TOTO: What happen to the queen?

PAPPYSHOW: The queen is combing her tresses. I bet you don't know what tresses is.

TOTO: I learn poetry in school, boy. [*recites*]
    Flaxen tresses crowned her head
    Her eyes so blue so we said
    She's a Nordic beauty alive not dead!

PAPPYSHOW [*placing the crown on his own head*]: You cannot hurry the queen.

ALL [*singing*]:
    Oh dear what can the matter be
    Dear dear what can the matter be
    Oh dear what can the matter be
    Jessie so long at the fair
    He promised to buy her a bunch of blue ribbons
    He promised to buy her a bunch of blue ribbons
    He promised to buy her a bunch of blue ribbons
    To tie up her bonnie brown hair.

MAKO: Year before I went to see the queen show in the savannah.

PAPPYSHOW [*like Bob Gittens, a radio commentator*]: And now we have contestant number nine, Miss Jestina Lewis. Height five feet seven inches. 34-32-34; hazel eyes, auburn tresses.

LAURA *looks at her watch.*

JESTINA [*before the mirror*]: This is the face to go and meet a man who is expecting an angel. This is the face to go with an say: This is your Jestina! This is your Jestina! Is me you been searching for all your life? This is that face?

PAPPYSHOW: Now over to June who will describe her dress.

LAURA: You . . . you ain't looking so bad.

JESTINA [*trying to make her understand*]: No. Tell me, somebody, a man, this man leave this island, he's a child seeking a better life . . . no, not a better life . . . seeking life, living, away from the drill and surviving of this place. And he gone. He gone. He is a moth on the highways of the whiteman land, seeking the light, feeling the fire, roasting

in the flaming coldness. And as he roasting, he turn and
find me. He find me. Jestina, he say: I coming home to
you. I tired with this place, tired chasing after a self that is
not here for me to find. I ain't have nothing again that I
want to prove to the whiteman . . . I coming home to you,
girl. To the cool sun in your thighs, to begin my life now
that I know it have life for me, to learn again to feel, to
touch, to bathe naked in the river, to drink again the water
of mountain springs. I coming home to you and to I. Tell
me, this man with all these strong hopes . . . I with this
face, I can go to him and say: Come let us bathe in the
river, let us drink together the waters of mountain springs.
I have no shame for myself, you think, I have no respect for
his feelings, for his dreams?

LAURA: But, but. But he see your photograph already. He know
how you look. You didn't send him a photograph of
yourself?

MAKO [*in American accent, as radio commentator at beauty show*]: Oh
and contestant number nine Jestina Lewis, Miss Jestina
Parlour is in a lovely, simply marvellous, a marvellously
stunning evening gown of pale beige chiffon studded with
diamantes, the dress is cut in an H line showing off her
lovely back . . . At the corners of her ears set off with
earrings . . . What lovely earrings . . .

LAURA: You didn't show me five photographs that you take out
yourself, and we went through them, you and me, and we
choose out the best one. The one with you stand up in the
botanic gardens near a palm tree when the immortelle was
blossoming and you agreed that yes that was the best one,
and you said yes I will send this one to him. Look, put on
the wig. What so different between your face and the one
in the picture? [JESTINA *takes the wig and looks at it
thoughtfully. She is composed, decisive.* MAKO *is finishing her
announcing. The rest of the crowd applauds wildly. The noise
reaches* JESTINA *and* LAURA. LAURA *speaks, with suspicion that
turns quickly to assurance*] You didn't send the photograph,
Jestina? Eh, Jestina? You didn't send it?

JESTINA: What you take me for? What everybody take me for? A iron wall? A rockstone mountain? A mad woman in truth? Look at me, thirty-nine years gone from my life already. And all my searching get me is this little parlour in this little village. So when this man, this chance, this hope . . . When I was ready to give up hope . . . When this man write and tell me he want a picture.

LAURA: You didn't send the picture, Jestina?

JESTINA: I look at the picture I had was to send. I look at the picture . . . I look at the picture. And I know how beautiful I is inside me. I know my beauty . . . And I look at my face in the mirror . . . I look at my face . . . [*from the crowd outside: uproarious laughter. The car horn blows*] Tell the car to go.

LAURA: Well, if you didn't send the picture, then you ain't have nothing to worry about. All you have to do is tell him you's Jestina.

JESTINA [*vexed with herself*]: I so foolish . . . I didn't have to send no picture. He didn't even ask for one, really. Hear what he say: He say, 'Jestina, I know how lovely you is. I know no photograph can capture your beauty, so don't send me a photograph special. Send some small thing that I could put in my wallet, hang on the wall where I shave in the morning, something, some small part of you.'

LAURA [*realizing*]: You coulda send him a ring, a chain, a leaf from a mango tree. You didn't have to send no picture.

JESTINA: I wanted to send a photograph.

LAURA [*surprised*]: You wanted to send a photo?

JESTINA: I wanted him to see me, to see my beauty. I wanted to give him something for him to take out his wallet and say to his friends: 'Look! Look at woman! Look at woman!' [*pause*] I wanted them to envy him.

PRETTYPIG [*outside*]: Year before I went to see queen show. The year when a girl in Afro win.

MAKO: Look how that stupidness gone outa fashion, eh.

DOCTOR: What?

TOTO: Afro, nuh. It was a style. That is all.

PRETTYPIG: Black girls does look good in Afro.

JESTINA: You see the picture he send? [*showing* LAURA *his picture*]
It is a picture of a warrior, a prince getting up off his knees.
I wanted to hold him up. I wanted to give him something
to boast about, to lift his chest up when he ploughed
through the snow . . . So I sent him a picture.

LAURA [*almost angrily*]: You coulda send him the one we
selected. You coulda write and tell him that you have had
a storm for a life and your photograph doesn't flatter you,
that you come through. You coulda tell him that: 'I have
survived.'

JESTINA [*sadly*]: You don't understand.

LAURA: The picture, the one you send, does it resemble you a
little bit? [*no reply*] You coulda say time passed, you
change a little. You was sick . . . That time has moved
greedily across your beauty.

JESTINA: But I am beautiful, Laura. I am beautiful. I am
beautiful.

LAURA [*excitedly*]: Tell him that. Come! [*trying to hurry her out
before she changes her mind again*] Go to him. Take these
flowers. They match your dress. Fix the wig. Tell him your
heart is a city of yellow lights, of orchids, of hibiscus in
bloom. Tell him.

JESTINA [*pushing her away*]: Get away from me! Leave me alone.

LAURA: You have to go [*with urgency and decisiveness*].

JESTINA [*collapsing*]: I make enough of a fool of myself already.

LAURA: You going to let him come this distance and not find
you? Have some faith in yourself, believe in your beauty.
Believe.

JESTINA [*the verge of surrender*]: Laura, I is a tired woman. Tired
of magic, of believing. Tired of battling this world with no
ammunition, tired labouring to find my note in the world
music. I is a bold, ridiculous woman. Mad woman Jestina
is the correct name for me. [*she goes to her drawer, opens it,
searches briefly and takes out a photo*]

PAPPYSHOW [*outside*]: You ain't notice that they cutting their
hair short like man own now. That is the style.

MAKO [*with lofty certainty*]: Long hair will always be in style.

JESTINA [*turning from the dresser, tears overwhelming her*]: You go, Laura. My courage and my truth can't change things. You go. Here! This is the picture I send him.

LAURA *takes the picture. Looks at it. Her countenance changes to alarm, astonishment.*

LAURA: Is my picture you send him? My picture?

JESTINA [*calm, almost accusing*]: You surprised?

LAURA: Why? You had no right!

JESTINA [*reproachful and explaining*]: It had to be yours. You don't see?

LAURA: You had no right.

JESTINA: It had to be yours.

TOTO [*from outside*]: I always feel them contest was for white girls.

JESTINA: Who else I could imitate? To be beautiful, to be a lady, I had to imagine myself you. You don't see. I had to put myself inside of you. In your house, with your parents and friends. You were my model, to walk well, to talk well, to sit. Remember when we were girls. I was the older, and before I knew . . . Before I knew that there was a me that I could become, I began to become you. My mother would point you out to me: 'See that little girl next door, see how sweetly she behaves; see that little girl next door, how lady-like she sits; see that little girl next door, how nice is her smile; see that little girl next door, how dainty is her walk; see that little girl next door! See that little girl next door?' [*her resentment increases, she becomes accusing*] You! I had to be you. Always from the beginning . . . It had to be your picture.

LAURA: You had no right. You had no right!

JESTINA: You inherited him, Laura, the same way you inherited your home and your parents and your dog and the piano that plays in your house. Accident. Luck. You inherited him. It's your face he's coming home to. Go and meet him. Go [*pushing her, she stops*]. I'll go with you. Just to see his face. I will be the friend that is envious. I'll hang in the back. He wouldn't know . . . [*ready to go. From outside, a long wailing cry of Jestina! The car horn blows*] Come on. The car outside blowing, and the foolish people calling my name.

LAURA [*reprimanding*]: Jestina, you had no right to send my picture, you know. You had no right, you know. Why must you come and give me this burden to carry again? Why? Why?

JESTINA: Because . . . you can bear it. Don't complain now. You didn't complain when they gave you the best parts in the school concert. You didn't complain out there in your flower garden tending flowers with gloves on, watching the young men dying at every swish of your dress tail. You didn't complain when they pick you to give bouquets to the dignitaries. You loved it, Laura. You loved it.

LAURA: I loved it? I loved it? I loved it? [*laughter and tears*]

JESTINA [*righteously*]: Don't cry for me. Not for me.

LAURA [*angrily*]: For you? Why for you? Why you believe you have a monopoly on the sorrow and pain of the world?

JESTINA: Pain? Sorrow? What do you know about pain?

LAURA: Do you know how it is for me, this life? Do you know?

PRETTYPIG [*outside*]: You know it had a time I didn't used to smile.

PAPPYSHOW: You lie.

PRETTYPIG: So help me, I didn't used to smile.

MAKO: Your teeth?

PRETTYPIG: No, not my teeth, my cheeks. They used to flare. Flare like a skirt.

LAURA: You know how it is, carrying this burden of being beautiful, when I don't even know what beauty is, walking through the narrow gate of this village pretending it's a palace and I am its queen. In prison here in this tomb of hypocrisy, pretence, afraid even to dream of escape far more plot it. Afraid to think, to feel, to be somebody for my own self. You know what this life is for me? Cry for you?

PAPPYSHOW [*outside*]: Red niggers was always in season.

LAURA: I have envied you your ugliness!

JESTINA: Envied me my ugliness! Laugh. Laugh, Laura. Laugh.

LAURA : I have envied you the freedom you had to be, to be a
failure, to be ugly, to be without talent or charm or grace,
to be vulgar and ignorant. [JESTINA *listens intently*] The
freedom you had to go out into the real world and move
and dance and feel hurt. Your freedom to experience and
to grow. How I longed to say to you: 'Jestina, take me with
you when you go out with those rough dangeous men who
would cuff you up and tumble you down. Take me
somewhere out of this safe prison. Let me dare too, let me
feel too.' Cry for you? I have been the prisoner.

JESTINA : But you loved it, Laura. You never said no to any of it,
you embraced it. I saw you with my eyes, at your parties,
on your verandah in the dim lights. [*she pauses*] Oh! You
feel he is not good enough for you, eh? Well, [*boastfully*], he
is educated too. He has his university degree. He is no
little pissin tail boy. He been away. Educated. He's not a
fool, you know. If you feel you too great for these boys
'round here, you not too great for him. He is a prince
returning to his country, to his throne, let me tell you; so
don't think you better than him.

LAURA [*wistfully*]: I didn't have the strength to admit to you, to
admit to myself, that it was all a lie: this pose of being
superior . . . I learned things from books . . . I learned
things by heart. I said them like a recitation, and made
you think I had invented them. So you see . . .

JESTINA : No, you lapped it up. All the praise and privileges it
brought you, you lapped it up. You never said no. [*loudly*]
You never said no.

LAURA : I could not. I was afraid.

JESTINA : And you let me go on believing in you all these years.
You let me go on holding you up as the image of what I
could become if I tried . . . if I learned to walk like you and
to talk like you and to pass my hand over my hair like you.
You knew your life wasn't real and you ain't say a word,
you let me go on believing in you. [*accusing*] You let me go
on?

LAURA [*wistfully as if to herself*]: When I was a girl, everybody
said I was so pretty. Everything I did was right, was

sacred. Like a kind of magic. I would wear ribbons in my
hair, and soon, all the little girls would wear ribbons in
their hair. I would comb my hair down, and they would
comb theirs down. And if theirs couldn't go down, they
would straighten it or curl it so it would be like mine. It
was a kind of magic.

JESTINA: You see, you coulda do anything you wanted.
Anything, Laura.

TOTO [*outside*]: One thing we could do is get dirty. My
grandmother used to tell my cousin: 'Brian, one thing, red
niggers can't be is dirty.'

LAURA [*pleading, explaining*]: But my responsibility, I had to set
an example. My father said: 'Laura, everybody is looking
at you.' You know what that is? You know what it is to live
your life as an example, when you don't know what life is
at all? You know what it is to live without no place to go,
no growing to do, just going over the same ground, being,
not becoming, no journeying, just repeating and
everybody looking at you?

JESTINA: You had everything.

LAURA: It was that every thing that imprisoned me. And it was
to see your eyes and hear your praise and feel your envy.

JESTINA: My praise! My envy! Yes, blame me again! Blame
me!

LAURA [*heatedly*]: Yes, your praise, your envy. You watched me.
You copied me.

JESTINA: Yes, I envied you. I copied you. Yes. You were the
only image of beauty in my world. Yes. You know what he
write and tell me?

LAURA: But you have lived for your own self, you have learnt for
yourself. You have been open, vulnerable. You have to put
your heart out there to be punched and your dreams to be
trampled. And you've kept on. You have lived, Jestina.

JESTINA: You know what he tell me, he say: 'I have gone
around the four corners of suffering. I am coming home,
Jestina, to the warm sun in your thighs, to the small rivers
where fish slide in new beginnings, to carrat houses and to
steam rollers to a land where we have not yet run out of

time, to feel in my bones the sea, the space that join our
islands.'

LAURA: Go to him, Jestina.

JESTINA: I am coming home to you, my green grasshopper
island that is still learning to fly. Coming home to your
firm breasts and to the valleys of your thighs still fertile for
planting, to sing with you in cool nights filled with the
sound of living, breathing things, not giving off the soot
and tar of engines.

LAURA: Don't blame me.

JESTINA: No, I don't blame you.

LAURA: Dammit, Jestina! Jestina, you are the truth. You are
still his island, with little rivers and carrat roofed houses
and the hills where parrots troop across the evenings. You
are the island with bamboos bent down and ready to rise
in another wind. You are here swayed, unbroken, you
have survived, Jestina.

JESTINA: Oh, what an island! What an island! My heart broken
by lovers, their names I do not even remember. My breasts
dragged down by centuries of bearing cane and coffee and
cocoa, sag now like landslides. Oh, what an island! The
marrow of my bones drained out like oil, pumped out,
syphoned to infuse another's heart. I am his island of
narrow men without dreams, without magic or song or
drum. I am his tired, forced ripe island that moves without
aim, without object, costuming my emptiness, in a
carnival band where you, your kind, the empty beauties
play the kings and queens. Yes, I am his island.

JESTINA *is sorrowful.*

LAURA: You are truth, Jestina. The true island.

JESTINA: Truth, truth is tired of her own beautiful ugliness. You
go to him. He has your picture. He is yours.

LAURA: NO. You go.

JESTINA: Your face will solve everything.

LAURA: What is a face?

JESTINA: What is a face? Surfaces. This world judges by

surfaces not by our hearts. [*half a hope*] You think I could
go to him and say I have lived, I have suffered, that I have
been cuffed and kicked by life and that this is how I look
now?

LAURA: He will understand. If he is the man you say he is.

JESTINA: No. [*resolutely*]

LAURA: I am a coward.

JESTINA: The world likes your kind of cowardice, your kind of
surviving that adds nothing to anything, that neither
lessens the world's pain nor increases its feelings. It is you
who are its statues, its nuns, its virgins, you who have not
been courageous enough to place an honest fart in one of
its buildings. He will choose you. I was wrong thinking
that maybe I had a chance that I could explain, but he will
choose you too. Go to him and smile. Take your earrings
and of course, you don't need a wig. Here is your flowers.

LAURA: What did you want me to do? Broadcast that my
beauty is a sham. Tell you that your ugliness is a lie. Yes,
it is a lie. Yes, it is a lie. It was always a lie. And you take
the lie and make it a defence. Your ugliness is a crutch.
Reach for your crutch now. Reach for it. Oh your face! Oh
your ugly face. Well, we are two cowards. You and me. So
don't blame me.

Outside: the noise of the crowd.

JESTINA [*becoming aware of herself, rising to full height, fixing herself,
rid now of all accessories*]: I am Jestina who you all laugh at
and ridicule for centuries. From school days all kinda
names you call me: 'Blackie Tropical, Picky head nanny,
Black tulum'.

LAURA [*defending*]: Yes feel sorry for yourself. Feel sorry.

JESTINA: And I walk with my head up. I walk with my head up
through the laughter. I walk in the road like a queen, I
standing up for years after you laugh me down and batter
me down, I still standing up for life, for living. I is a queen.
You hear me. I, Jestina, is a queen. And that man who
coming home, my warrior, my man, my prince. I will go to

him on bended knees. I will go and I will say to him:
[*pause*] 'Welcome, Prince, returning from the far
continents of suffering. Welcome, my warrior, returning to
your hut in the thighs of your woman.' And I will part my
veil and I will say to him: 'This is what they have done
with me. This is what I have become over the centuries.
Yes. This is your queen. Let me wash your wounds with
my lips of waiting. Let my tears of gladness bathe your
feet.' And he would say to me: 'Rise, my woman. Rise up,
my queen. Let us be done with pitiful cries of affliction.
Let us be done with the diseased laughter of our agony.
Let us rise up to our beginning to the space for us to grow
in.' And he would lift me with his hands up on my feet and
he would look at my face and like the lover he is, my prince
would kiss me. I am going to him. Come, Laura, come
with me. [*She steps out regally, with wig, etc. The crowd giggles.
They begin to eye each other and laugh*]. Giggle, you fools.
Giggle, mock, for you are defeated. [*the crowd falls into a
hush.* LAURA *takes her arm to guide her to the car whose horn is
blowing*]. They have whipped you. They have turned you
into their own worst enemy. They have made you the
jailers of your own prison. So poison yourselves with your
ridicule. Kill yourselves with your grinning laughter.
Watch me and envy me, for long after the last poor one of
you suffocate in the vomit of your cowardice, long after the
echoes of your laughter dies, I shall be walking still,
striding still, with my head up against the winds of the
world, battling to become myself. So laugh on bretheren,
laugh. [*they begin to sing: 'Go way Jestina, who go married to
you'.* JESTINA *starts to hum and join their dancing*]. I am going to
meet my lover. He is tall as a mountain and strong. I am
alive, I am daring, moving, so laugh! Laugh! [*she dances*]
LAURA: Don't dance with them. Don't. Hold your strength.
You are the pillars of temples and the axles of wheels. You
are the spars of long ships and the paving of avenues that
run across the face of cities. You are the truth.
JESTINA: I am not afraid of these insects, Laura. I can dance
with them. [*dancing*] They cannot touch me. I can dance.
Dance! Dance! Dance! Laura dance!

LAURA *tries to pull her away.*

LAURA: No. Let us go.
JESTINA: I do not have to hide from them. I do not have to be
    ashamed of living.
LAURA: We will be late.
JESTINA: I want you to come with me. Laura, you will come eh?
LAURA: Yes.
JESTINA: Let him see you. Then I will explain.
LAURA: Yes. [*tugs her away*]

They exit. JESTINA *dancing. The crowd continues to sing and dance.*

Act Two

The street outside JESTINA *'s house/parlour. The same group assembled.*

MAKO : I tell you it woulda happen so.

PRETTYPIG : I hear police nearly lock she up.

DOCTOR : Lock she up?

PRETTYPIG : Poor thing!.

PAPPYSHOW [*assertive, vindictive, triumphant*] : Poor thing my arse!
    She was too blasted bold. Too brave, to think she could
    walk just so with that face through the world.

MAKO : I can't blame the man, though.

TOTO : He come?

PRETTYPIG : But ain't the man did promise to marry her?

PAPPYSHOW : The world did make a more wicked promise to her
    long before his own.

PRETTYPIG [*sympathetically*] : He shouldn't'ta do she that
    though . . . If was me . . .

TOTO : If was you, and if was me, it wouldn't'ta have no trouble.
    We woulda have we wedding and we cake sticking, and I'd
    a lift you over the trestle like them star boys in pictures . . .
    [*moving towards her, making to lift her up, a grin on his face*]
    Lemme see how heavy you is. Lemme see.

PRETTYPIG *just watches him sternly, and he retreats.*

DOCTOR [*more to himself than to the others*] : We wouldn't learn, eh.
    We keep on going through the world with hope, with
    dreams. Is like they put we so . . . So why this poor woman
    have to go out looking for magic to happen, for man to
    change from the beast he is? Why? Why we have to keep
    on going as if anybody care bout love or truth or pain?
    [*looking around*] Unless we have in we some kinda Jehovah
    Witness Shango Baptist Christian faith to get up again
    and walk; like Lazarus, who refuse to dead though they
    put him in the grave.

TOTO : What really happen? The man come? I thought they say

he jump back on the plane when he see Jestina face.

MAKO [*with authority*]: Is her fault. She can't blame a soul. I
mean, Jestina coulda well put on the wig and make up she
face; but no: Princess Jestina go to meet him just so . . .

PAPPYSHOW: With she face hard as iron, and the veins stand out
on she hands.

TOTO: So he come then?

PRETTYPIG: And the man? Nice?

MAKO: So-so.

PAPPYSHOW: He was a nice man: like me so. With his hair on
his head in a big Afro. And his chest bare at the neck of his
dashiki, pacing [*he reshapes his clothing, the better to become the
man, steps away from the group, the visitor entering the airport
lounge, looking around, searching*] . . . pacing the halls of the
airport, like a lion just out the winter of a New York zoo.
[*he walks, overplaying it*].

MAKO [*still telling the story*]: So the man, when he spot them . . .

TOTO: Them?

MAKO: I didn't tell you? The fool [*nudging* PRETTYPIG] . . . The
fool carry Laura with she.

PRETTYPIG: Oh Gord!

MAKO: You find a man, hide him away. Is not to say she don't
know this place. They will take away anything from you.

DOCTOR: And not because they want it. But because they could
deprive you of it. Is a kinda raff and scramble we grow up
in. In war days, the Yankees used to throw sweetie in the
air for children to rush and scramble for. We used to rush
and half kill one another, and we don't know if is a bomb
fold up in the sweetie paper.

TOTO: Grab, yes. How else you going to get anything?

DOCTOR [*solemnly*]: It does vex me, though. It show no respect
for the noble among us, or for the nobleness in us. Is like
we saying that nobody ain't having no taller spirit, no
greater pride: that all o we is one: equal pigs in equal sties.
And you does get like a pig, like a animal. One Friday
evening, I rushing for a bus. Rushing, rushing for a bus.
And when I finish rush, elbowing women, trampling
children, my shirt tear, and my ear bell ringing from

where I get a cuff, I now asking the driver where the bus going. Arima . . . I was going Couva. So I went Arima, I was so shame.

TOTO [*assertively*]: I is a Russian when it come to rushing. This is Trinidad, and if you want to get anything that is yours, or get any place that you are going, you don't stay back unless you is a invalid.

PAPPYSHOW [*impatient for the story, theatrical*]: Look! I here at the airport. Let me hear what . . . As you was saying . . .

MAKO : Well, she carry Laura with she. So since is Laura picture the man have, is Laura he will go to.

TOTO [*triumphant, as if vindicated*]: So is Laura picture the bitch send. Ah-h! I know she didn't have the guts. I know she didn't have the blasted guts.

The others are entering their roles. PAPPYSHOW *moves to embrace* MAKO.

PAPPYSHOW : Jestina! [*embracing, lifting, whirling her around — actually,* PAPPYSHOW *is using the occasion to get in a free hug on* MAKO] Oh home! Oh island! Ah sun! How sweet oh Lord to be here, to be home. How sweet to leave New York cold and come home to my island, my woman, my sun. How sweet! Amen! Amen! [*bends and kisses the ground, embraces* MAKO *again*]

MAKO [*cutting eyes at* PAPPYSHOW]: Is just show we showing. It ain't real, you know.

PAPPYSHOW : I real.

PRETTYPIG : Our sons, our lovers, are returning, tall as pouis, to stand in the sun, to blaze on our hillsides, to bring rain. To bring rain [*moving as if wanting to embrace* PAPPYSHOW, *but restraining herself*]

PAPPYSHOW : Well, let's go. [*snaps his fingers at the porter,* DOCTOR] Hey! Hey!

DOCTOR [*grumbling. He doesn't move*] Hey? Hey? [*savouring the words*] Is so they does talk to people. Hey! As soon as they go away and come back. Hey! Hey! Hey!

MAKO : Don't bother with him. Insolence is eating out their insides. They do not want to work. You have to beg them.

PAPPYSHOW [*bowing, overplaying*]: Brother, I'm sorry. If I
    offended you, I apologize. I just wanted to get my bags.
    And seeing you there as if you were waiting, to serve, to
    work, I thought . . .
DOCTOR [*righteous and dismissive*]: Awright! Awright! Awright!
    Where you going? I busy.
PAPPYSHOW [*amazed and pained*]: Brother, we have time to live.
    Brother, we have time for each other.
MAKO: Leave him alone. We'll get another one.
DOCTOR [*challengingly, impatiently*]: Where you going, man?
PAPPYSHOW: Brother, we have time in this world. I'm telling
    you, man. We have time.
DOCTOR [*sucking his teeth, grumbling*]: Talking shit. Don't even
    know where he going . . . Hey?
PAPPYSHOW: All I said was Hey. [*astonished — to the women*]
PRETTYPIG: It is our powerlessness. The strength we have is in
    our resentment. In our sullenness. You must be gentle
    with them. They're fragile like Ti Marie trees, breathe on
    them, they close their leaves and expose their thorns.
PAPPYSHOW: All I said was Hey.
MAKO: Don't worry with him. You'll soon be away from such
    people [*dismissing*].
PAPPYSHOW: Away from them? [*police sirens blare, sounds of
    commotion, gunshots*. PAPPYSHOW *looks around him*] Man, this is
    New York!
MAKO: You won't have to put up with them. Not with your
    qualifications. Thank God, you'll be away in St Ann's
    Gardens, Ellerslie Park or one of those nice suburban
    hillsides. With your qualifications they will give you a
    good job. You'll live away from them. You won't have to
    see such. [*she flicks her hands disdainfully at* DOCTOR]
PRETTYPIG: A job? What will you do with a job? You didn't
    have a job for four hundred years. You don't feel we had
    enough jobs, enough yes sir; yes sir, saying what we think
    they want to hear, making ourselves what we think they
    want us to become. Haven't we had enough jobs with
    them?

PAPPYSHOW: Them? Are they still here? [*seems surprised, even frightened*]

MAKO [*quickly, reassuringly*]: Of course . . . It's not like long ago. Here, every creed and race . . .

PAPPYSHOW: All of we is still one? Still one?

MAKO: All of we is one. We can't change. Is so we are: multi-racial, not like in South Africa. You know, people come from all over the world to study us. They want to know how we manage to live so still. Oh, yes, we can't go to the moon, but we can teach them how people should live. We can teach the world.

PAPPYSHOW But I . . . I thought . . . Black Power, Independence, Black Governor General, President, Republic. I thought . . . We . . .

PRETTYPIG: We are still waiting to begin. That is why we are so happy to see you.

PAPPYSHOW: But, I . . . I could have sworn . . .

MAKO: Of course, Black Power came; and marched and marched. Some of us had to stay indoors. If I tell you how frightened I was. I refused to walk down the streets of Port of Spain. But, you know, they were right. They had a grouse, and they marched it out of their system. I think it helped all of us. People got benefits. But how can you benefit if you are not qualified? [*this is her big point*]

PRETTYPIG: Qualified?

PAPPYSHOW: I have my BA, and my MA, and I'm going back for my PhD. They can't say I'm not qualified.

PRETTYPIG: Qualified! [*she looks first at* PAPPYSHOW, *then* MAKO, *nudging* MAKO] Tell him.

PAPPYSHOW: But, somehow, I thought . . .

MAKO: Things have really opened up for people with qualifications.

PAPPYSHOW: But we have had qualified people. Technicians. Years of scholarship winners studying in the best Universities. They should be running things.

MAKO: But, they are. They have nice jobs. Nice, nice jobs. Alexander, a boy I know, going round with a friend of mine . . . Rushin . . . you mightn't know him: he's now

quite big. But, you know, here and there is a little
prejudice. Alex wouldn't stand for it. We get the highest
jobs now. All over.

PRETTYPIG: Tell him.

MAKO [*with a glance, signals* PRETTYPIG *to wait*]: Oh, and the
place is fine. I wouldn't live anywhere else if they paid me.
Everywhere has its problems. Aren't there problems in
New York?

Enter TOTO, *a mad looking, dada head, grimy fellow. He had been
sitting in silence all the time.*

TOTO [*to* PAPPYSHOW]: Gimme a cigarette. [*his eyes fierce*]

PAPPYSHOW [*astounded by the threat and insolence*]: Why?

TOTO *glares at him long. Then begins to move off. He turns back.*

TOTO: Like you vex that I ask you for a cigarette. [*threateningly*]

PAPPYSHOW: Yes.

PRETTYPIG: Give him. Give him the cigaretee.

PAPPYSHOW: Is how you ask me, man. Is how you ask me . [*he
takes a pack from pocket*] Here! [*handing it to* TOTO] Take the
pack. Is how you ask me, man. Is how he ask me [*turning to
the women*].

TOTO *takes the cigarette and moves off.*

PRETTYPIG: Tell him [*louder, to* MAKO].

PAPPYSHOW [*turning from gazing at the retreating* TOTO]: Tell me
what?

MAKO [*combative, asserting status, exasperation in her tone*]: Tell him
what?

PRETTYPIG: I am Jestina! [*pauses, looks for response*] It is I who
been writing you all these years, who have been waiting all
these centuries for you to come home. I . . . Me. Tell him,
Laura!

PAPPYSHOW: Jestina? She? She?

MAKO [*superior*]: She's a crazy woman they call Mad Jestina,

from the village. I talked a lot about you. She begged to
come with me.

PRETTYPIG [*surprised*]: Laura? Laura? [*pleading*] Laura!

MAKO: Now she decide that you came to her. Can you believe
it?

PAPPYSHOW: Miss . . .? Madam?

PRETTYPIG: I know you will ask why: if I am Jestina, why do I
wear this face when you came expecting another?

PAPPYSHOW [*with sympathy he cannot afford*]: Yes. Yes. Why have
you come with that face?

MAKO: She lives next door to me. She's known me for years.
Her mother was the maid in our house. I guess I talked too
much about you.

PRETTYPIG: I was weak. I was ashamed. I was frighten. I felt
that you would not be able to like me, that you would not
be able to accept me. I didn't want to take the chance that
you would think me ugly in comparison. I knew you
wanted beauty. I knew you were in competition. You
needed a representative, someone that compared with
them, on their grounds. And though I know the truth, I
didn't trust presenting it to you . . . You see, I didn't trust
you.

MAKO [*glancing at* PAPPYSHOW]: Oh!

PRETTYPIG [*an appealing cry*]: I didn't disrespect you. I know the
powers, the forces, the images that have moulded you. I
was trying to protect you, to protect me, to protect us. I
didn't want you to reject me before you understood me,
before you got to know my beauty.

PAPPYSHOW: So that's why you sent me her [*pointing*] picture?

MAKO: That's why you sent my picture?

PRETTYPIG: You see, when you asked me for something to
remember me by . . . You remember that letter? When
you . . . When I realized that you wanted a picture, I
thought . . . And then that was some years ago when all I
had was a faith, a hope, that somehow I could be a person.
You must remember I lived in a world they ruled. You see,
I, we, all of us, we could not claim ourselves because we
didn't have the power to affirm ourselves. I was what they
allowed me to be, what they required that I be. They

confused me. They dominated me. I did not think my own
thoughts. I thought what I felt they wanted me to think. I
behaved how I felt they would approve. I wanted to look
how they looked. It is true. Only in the most private area
of myself I felt there was a me. You see, it was not for
myself that I was myself but for them. I felt only in the
most private way that I was a person: that's why I had to
split myself in two.

MAKO [*hollowly*]: Ha! Ha! In two.

PRETTYPIG: In two. I believed that I could be beautiful on the
inside, and ugly outside. There were two truths I had to
live: my ugliness and my beauty. Two truths. How could I
send you these two truths? I hid what I thought I had to
hide, what I thought was my ugliness, so I sent you one
truth, and a picture that I thought would express it.
[PAPPYSHOW *looks suspiciously at her*. PRETTYPIG *tugs at his
sleeves, hurrying, feeling the need to explain*] It is like some of the
letters I wrote you about the island. I told you about
carnival, the beaches, the bamboos on river banks, the
immortelle in the valleys: things that would please you.
Truths that were pleasant. I did not tell you about the
strikes, the marches, the poverty, the corruption of youth,
and the dying of living things, and the emptiness, the deep
emptiness of our existence. I told you what I had practice
telling: one of the truths. Then you wrote me another
letter that plucked me like a guitar string and left me
trembling with this note, this hope. You said: 'Truth will
have the last word, the alpha and omega, for it is always
there like a tender plant beneath the decaying folds of the
lies we see'. You said that.

MAKO [*uneasy*]: She has this . . . this fantastic memory.

PRETTYPIG: I have been trembling ever since, waiting for you,
trying to hold on to the self that they had made bastard in
myself, waiting for us to begin in the ugly beautifulness of
our truth. I didn't know how to explain about the letter. I
thought you'd come and discover me yourself, that you
would see me and care, out of your own self. Truth would
be our beginning.

MAKO: Dreams, fantasies. She has these . . . these fantasies:
Someone sweeping her off magically . . . On a white
charger, like in a fairy tale.

PAPPYSHOW: Magically?

MAKO: Our people believe in magic; the sudden ascension, the
parting of the Red Sea, the immediate lottery, Cinderella.

PRETTYPIG [*crying out*]: No. No. No. Magic cannot save me,
cannot save us. We cannot be catapulted into a new world;
we have to begin, with truth. That is why I threw away the
wig and came with this face. If we have to begin at all, to
be able to grow at all, to have a self at all, we must begin
with the truth.

PAPPYSHOW: Of your appearance?

PRETTYPIG: You have the power to make me myself. By
accepting me, you can make me beautiful. For beauty is
. . . beauty is . . . truth . . . affirmed. You have the power.
What else is our promise? Our hope? After your
journeyings, you can't come back home to deal in the same
old lies, to see in the same old way. [PAPPYSHOW *appears
confused, looks to* MAKO *as if for help*] You can't come back
here to get a job to seek the magic of a Hollywood
romance, to live the old lie of our living, to uphold the very
images that by comparison made you ugly. You can't
come back for that. You come back to begin with the
truth; for you cannot know beauty . . . until . . . you know
truth. You . . . your letters made me live again. I am the
guitar string still tingling with the sound you tugged from
me.

PAPPYSHOW *seems impressed, glances at* MAKO *almost helplessly.*

MAKO [*superior, but faltering a bit, loud, anxious*]: If . . . if . . . [*she
tries to laugh*] If you are the truth, do you think we can bear
that truth? Can we bear the obnoxious porter and the
grimy bum? Can we bear the bullying sullenness of these
people? I mean, if your truth is so ugly, can you ask
anyone to bear it, to embrace it?

PRETTYPIG: Truth can never be too ugly when truth is you.

[PAPPYSHOW, *confused, sighs*]. I have waited on you. I have
waited. All through your journeys, your disasters, your
defeats. I've watched you walk, your chest swollen with
pride and shame, and you wouldn't take my hand. I hid in
corners, in beauty parlours, trying to become the woman I
thought pleased you, knowing I could not claim you, that
you could not claim me. But now you are here. You have
come home. You have come home to your native land.

PAPPYSHOW [*in a sort of daze*]: I have come home. I have come
home.

PRETTYPIG: You have come home. I am your beginning. [*steps
forward with a frightening boldness*] Don't jump into the
middle of this dying, killing, stream, begin. Let me help
you search. Let me listen to your rage, when you rage. Let
my body be the field of your fantasies. Let us rewrite our
histories. Let me be your friend.

PAPPYSHOW [*alarmed*]: Who . . . Who is she? Who is she?

MAKO [*sharply, alarmed too*]: I tell you, she's a mad woman. Mad
Jestina living next to me.

PRETTYPIG: And I lonely too. Let us be friends. Let me learn to
understand you and to trust you. Teach me! Learn me
your dreams before you forget them, recall for me those
you are beginning to forget, so that in an evening when
you crouch, bend, in the harshness of their dying day . . .
when they overwhelm you I will recite them to you to
make you strong again.

PAPPYSHOW: Who is she?

PRETTYPIG: Be my warrior. Let me strengthen you with my
caring; let me arm you with my love. Let us fling ourselves
into our beginning. [MAKO *holds* PAPPYSHOW*'s arm. He is
looking at* PRETTYPIG] You know why I came with this face?
It is because there is no more time for lies, for getting
through, for sliding by. We are grown now. The burden of
our living is ours, not the whiteman's. I hoped, I believed
that you would be able to look at me and say: This is my
woman. This is my island with the bruises and sagging
breasts, with the teeth marks of soucouyants on her thighs,
still standing after the rapes: this is my love, the beautiful

old battleaxe with her nose twisted by the ungloved fists of
her captors and the traitors' knife scars in her back. I
believed in you.

PAPPYSHOW: You? You believed in me?

PRETTYPIG: I believed in you. [*with touching earnestness*]

PAPPYSHOW *feels the tug of her truth*. MAKO *is getting frantic*

MAKO [*loudly*]: Enough! Enough! Let's go [*tugging* PAPPYSHOW].
You must be tired after your trip. Constable! Constable!

PRETTYPIG [*with dignity and sincerity*]: I believed in you. I
believed that you were warrior enough, with strength
enough, and beauty and tallness to lift me from my bended
knees and part my veil and see my face and say, 'Come,
my woman, come, my queen'. [*anxious now*] I believed in
you.

MAKO [*breathless*]: Constable! Constable!

The Constable, TOTO, *comes over and looks them over enquiringly*.

MAKO [*breathless still*]: Constable, this woman is molesting us,
you hear!

PRETTYPIG: I believed that you would have the love and faith
and courage to seek yourself and find me in yourself, the
calm truth to break away from all the lies heaped on your
life time and begin.

MAKO: Constable, I tell you, this woman is molesting us.

PRETTYPIG: They did not give you a scholarship. They did not
send you abroad. You do not have to prove nothing to
them. You do not have to go to Ellerslie Park for them. No
one will miss you there. Don't you see, it's better so. You
have no scholarship, no promissory note, to serve lies and
deceit. That frees you. You are free. You are free! Don't
you see!

TOTO: Miss . . . Madame, the lady say you disturbing her and
her husband.

MAKO: My fiancé.

TOTO: Her fiancé.

MAKO : Making obscene proposals to my fiancé.

TOTO : Making obscene proposals to her fiancé.

PRETTYPIG : You are free!

MAKO [*aggressively*]: Officer, I will not put up with this, you
  know. What's your number?

TOTO [*to* PRETTYPIG]: Madame!

MAKO *tries to tug* PAPPYSHOW *away, but he stands looking at*
PRETTYPIG.

PRETTYPIG : Free, to become yourself, to become you . . . And
  you will go?

TOTO [*touching* PRETTYPIG]: Madame!

MAKO : Officer, drag her away! Take her down! Don't you see
  she mad.

TOTO [*touching* PRETTYPIG]: Madame, I'm speaking to you.

PRETTYPIG [*whirls upon* TOTO]: You see! [*looking at* PAPPYSHOW]
  You see! Is bacchanal they want. Bacchanal. To
  scandalize yourself, to bring yourself down, like a jamette.
  [*screaming*] To raise up your dress and show them your
  panty. [*turning to* TOTO *screaming still*] Did you, you idiot,
  see me disturbing this co-called lady? Did you? Everybody
  is a jamette to all you . . . everybody.

TOTO [*toughening*]: You talking to me?

PRETTYPIG : Who the hell you think I talking to? You just stand
  up there waiting to do their bidding, to run at the flutter of
  their eyelids and the lifting of their fine voices. I am talking
  to you, policeman.

TOTO [*turning away smiling*]: This woman mad, yes.

PRETTYPIG : Yes, sir, I mad. I mad. [MAKO *holds* PAPPYSHOW *by the
  arm. They turn now as if to leave, disturbed by the commotion.*
  PRETTYPIG *rushes to* PAPPYSHOW] You going? You going? You
  black son of a bitch, I believed in you.

PAPPYSHOW : I . . . I don't know you. Your face. I don't know
  that face.

PRETTYPIG [*grabbing hold of him*]: I am your Jestina. I am your
  woman. [PAPPYSHOW *turns to go.* PRETTYPIG *holds him still, first
  around his waist, then as he walks, her hands slip down to legs. She*

drags on the ground as he walks away] I believed in you. I
believed in you. I knew you had the strength, the truth, the
beauty. I believed, Oh God, that you would not fail me,
that you would be man, warrior, prince.

MAKO [*beckoning*]: Porter! Porter! We have some bags. Come,
help us. [*to* PAPPYSHOW] You see. She is mad. Come quickly
before you get yourself involved.

PAPPYSHOW *prises* PRETTYPIG*'s hands off his ankles, shakes his leg,
moves off. They exit,* MAKO *calling the porter.* TOTO *comes over to*
PRETTYPIG *who is lying on the ground.*

TOTO: Madame.
PRETTYPIG: Lock me up! Lock me up! I mad in truth. [*crying*]
TOTO: Madame, Get up! Come! Get up! [*gently*]

She looks at TOTO *with a blank stare and begins to rise. The players are
back to themselves.* PAPPYSHOW *is thoughtful. He has a little half smile
on his face.*

MAKO [*assertively*]: She was mad.
DOCTOR: She had to be mad.
PRETTYPIG: You think she was really mad?
TOTO: If she was really what?
PRETTYPIG: I mean . . . I don't know.
MAKO: Well, they coulda do it different.
TOTO: Do what different? You woulda leave Laura for she?
You woulda leave Ellerslie Park fort Shanty Town?
Tresses for pickey head?
PRETTYPIG: But if you did know. If you had love. If you believed
that it was a beginning.
DOCTOR: Who wants to begin? Everybody want to grow up big.
Who the hell wants to begin?
PAPPYSHOW [*composure regained, uproarious laughter*]: I believed in
you! I believed in you [*mimicking* JESTINA]. She was mad no
arse. She was mad [*absolute certainty*].

The women sing funeral slow. Singing continues in the background as

JESTINA *walks by with long white dress, hibiscus in her hair.*

> Go way, Jestina, who go married to you?
> Go way, Jestina, who go married to you?
> Go way, Jestina, who go married to you?
> Cause your face like a whale
> 'Like you just come from jail!
>
> Oh what a disgrace
> When I look at Jestina face
> Water in my eye
> Woman you make me cry
> She must be mad
> To believe that in Trinidad
> A woman like she
> Could wrangle matrimony.

PAPPYSHOW [*continuing*]: Go 'way Jestina. Aye, Jestina. Where the man? Where him?

TOTO [*holding his crotch*]: You ugly bitch! Is man you want?

DOCTOR: Leave her alone, man. You don't understand suffering? [*they laugh*] You don't understand feeling. Ease her up, man. Ease her up.

PAPPYSHOW [*aggressively*]: Ease her up?

DOCTOR: She feeling, man. Ease her up.

The others momentarily seem touched.

PAPPYSHOW: Toto, I didn't know Doctor still had uses for woman. Doctor, you feel you could take that on?

TOTO [*to* DOCTOR]: Put a bag over she face and you easy.

DOCTOR: Ease her up.

PAPPYSHOW [*loudly, with authority*]: Why the arse I must feel sorry for she? What sorry could do?

DOCTOR: We have to learn to feel, man.

PAPPYSHOW *laughs at* DOCTOR.

TOTO: Feel for what? All she want is a stiff prick.

Uproarious laughter.

PAPPYSHOW [*laughing and hailing loudly, vulgarly*]: Jestina, where
    the man?
JESTINA: You black mudder arse! [*with a kind of tall calm, she
    approaches them*] Watch me and laugh. Laugh. I am the ugly
    duckling, the swan, the queen, who only a prince could
    kiss and turn into a princess. But they ain't make the man
    yet, with the love yet, and the courage and the beauty to
    get me. So kiss my arse. All you hear me. Kiss my arse.
    [*lifts up her dress, points her bottom, and screams as they all laugh
    uneasily*]

Lights go down slowly as PAPPYSHOW *and group restrained, reflective,
almost sad, sing:*

> Jestina, girl,
> Who go married to you?
> Jestina, girl,
> Who go married to you?
> [*Repeat*]
> For your face is like a whale
> Like you just come from jail
> [*Chorus*]
> Oh what a disgrace
> When I look at Jestina's face.
> Water in my eye
> Woman you make me cry
> She must be mad
> To believe that in Trinidad
> A woman like she
> Could wrangle matrimony.

CURTAIN

The New Hardware Store

Play in Two Acts

Dedicated to Beverley Aleong

The New Hardware Store was first performed by the UWI Players on 21-2 and 27-9 March, 1980 with the following cast:

A A ABLACK, Rawle Harriot
ROOSO, Finbar Ryan
MISS CALLISTE, E. Ann Henry
MISS PRIME, Ann Marie Joseph
Directed by Gregory McGuire
Stage Manager, Keith Carter

Characters

A A ABLACK, hardware store manager and owner
ROOSO, his advertiser and nightwatchman
MISS CALLISTE, his bookkeeper
MISS PRIME, his typist

Act One

When the audience enters the theatre, ROOSO, *in his advertiser's outfit, is in the lobby, distributing handbills that advertise the store. Blaring calypso music accompanies him.* ROOSO *is in his forties. Over a clown suit, two placards hang from his shoulders, one on his back and the other on his chest. The placards read:*

> *A A ABLACK*
> *HARDWARE STORE FOR A CHANGE*
> *IMPORTED LUMBER, GALVANIZE,*
> *LOCAL, IMPORTED CEMENT, NAILS,*
> *LAMINATE SHEETS, BLOCKS PLYWOOD,*
> *SANITARY FITTINGS, STEELRODS,*
> *WROUGHT IRON AND OTHER HARDWARE ITEMS*

ROOSO [*speaking through a megaphone*]: A A Ablack hardware store. You have been waiting on it. Now it's here to satisfy your needs for building, renovating, repair. Our twenty-four-hour delivery service will bring deliverance to builders; our carnival prices will make your worries disappear; padlocks, bolts, wrought iron. We offer security to citizens of our nation. Build with Ablack and you build strong. Build with Ablack and you build a nation.

The audience is seated. From the stage hard heavy rockers music. Lights go up on the interior of a hardware store located on East Independence Square, Port of Spain. Apart from hardware supplies, there is a swinging door to the Manager's office on which, in disproportionately large letters, is written 'Manager'. Chair and desk for typist and the same for clerk. A set of flags and buntings that have begun to fade. A large framed photograph of MR ABLACK *taken ten years earlier. About the store itself is a mood not so much of disintegration as of lack of a central theme. Numerous signs about work, cleanliness, punctuality, success, contradict each other.*

   MISS CALLISTE, *the bookkeeper, is at her desk, copying figures from bills and writing them into a ledger. She is in her thirties. Still an*

*attractive woman, she has now become less interested in her appearance,
has little make-up, undistinguished clothes.*

The Manager's door opens and out of it emerges, very importantly,
MISS PRIME. *She is 18. She has about her that briskness and energy of her
age, very smartly dressed, made up to look like the model she would like to
become. She is very self-conscious of her appearance and is not as alert as
she might be to her surroundings and the people around her. She stands a
moment at the door and* MR ABLACK, *the Manager and owner of the
store, joins her. She is very attentive as he speaks to her, sending her to
summon* ROOSO. *Then she marches offstage with her self-conscious
importance.* ABLACK *now turns to* CALLISTE. ABLACK *is in his forties.
He is neatly dressed in a shirtjack suit, wearing a gold ring on one finger,
a gold identification band on one wrist and a heavy wristwatch on the
other. His well-groomed appearance is beginning to wear thin, but he
presents, if not a successful appearance, one of some solidity and self-
confidence. He is already irritated when he enters, and the loud music
irritates him further, but he has learned to control himself.*

ABLACK: Miss Calliste, the wrought iron reach yet?

CALLISTE: Not yet, Mr Ablack.

ABLACK: Where, where is Sam?

CALLISTE: Sam in the back stacking up the plywood.

ABLACK: Look, when the wrought iron reach, get Sam to put a
few lengths in front by the door.

CALLISTE: By the door, Mr Ablack? [*she pauses for him to realize
the error of such a course*] People wouldn't trip on them?

ABLACK [*with his own sense of wisdom*]: Let him tie a red cloth on
the ends. I want people to see that we have wrought iron
back in stock. For two weeks we didn't have none. We
don't want to lose our reputation for offering security to
the nation. People need wrought iron not only for
foundation, but to make barrication for doors, windows,
louvres. Today building is not shelter, it is fortification.

CALLISTE [*rising*]: I'll tell Sam right away.

ABLACK: And that rockers music, that dread rasta music that
Sam playing whole day. His player hook into my
electricity? Is my current it hook in to? Because if is my
electricity . . .

CALLISTE [*somewhat defensively*]: Sam, I think, does bring his own
    batteries.
ABLACK: And tell Sam to move a little faster. We have deliveries
    to make. He not working for Laquis, he working for
    Ablack. [CALLISTE *exits just as* PRIME *returns, a little hurriedly as
    if in fear of pursuit.* ABLACK *already anticipating trouble*] And
    Rooso?
PRIME: I gave him your message.
ABLACK [*anticipatory, almost aggressive*]: And what he tell you?
    [*she seems reluctant to speak*] What he tell you?

Enter ROOSO *up an aisle of the theatre, his voice overloud in the habitual
way he speaks to himself while letting those concerned know what he is
thinking.*

ROOSO: That is why I tell them: Take me out the storeroom!
    Take me out the storeroom. Because every minute
    somebody calling me: Rooso! Run for the table! Rooso,
    that lady ain't pay, catch her for me. Up and down like a
    jackass without owner; I don't know where I is. I leave the
    storeroom so I could be on my own. So I could be free, in a
    way. Yet no day I can't get a rest. No day.
ABLACK [*who has been anxiously waiting for him, sharply*]: Rooso,
    you don't see a car in the parking lot? You don't know that
    the parking lot is for customers? How you could just let
    people drive in and park and they not buying here?
ROOSO: So you want me to go out there and give him a ticket,
    since I is your police force? Or maybe you want me to do
    investigative work. A secret agent to follow people around
    and find out if they buying here, before I give them the
    ticket?
ABLACK: But you right outside there, man. You right out there
    where you could see what going on. And is like I don't
    have nobody out there. Is like anybody could come in and
    do what the hell they like, like the place is a republic.
ROOSO [*warning*]: Mr Ablack.
ABLACK [*aggressive, ready*]: Eh? Eh? What?
ROOSO: Mr Ablack. Mr Ablack, I tell you already, I can't do

two job in one. In the day I is the advertiser for this store.
My job is to go out on the pavement and walk about with
these two placard on my back.

ABLACK: And nothing else matters? Nothing else, eh? Eh?

ROOSO: People look at me like I mad; but this is my wuck. I
don't mind it. In this country you have to be mad to be
free.

ABLACK [*sarcastic*]: You very free.

ROOSO: Anyway, Shakespeare say the world is a stage. I is a
player. I ain't vex. This part fall on me. I get ketch.
Karma, the Hindus say. And if you watch me move, and
listen to me, you will see I does play it good . . . Listen to
all the advertisers it have in Port of Spain: it ain't have one
to punctuate with me. I could say, A A Ablack Hardware
store for a change. I could say, A! A! Ah Black Hardware
store for a change. I could say, A! A! Ah Black! And
surprise everybody. I could shape the message anyhow I
want, and for you, that is money. I could rattle off:
Imported lumber, galvanize, local and imported, laminate
sheets, nails, blocks, plywood, sanitary fittings, wrought
iron; and make people who ain't even have a spot to build
on come in and pay down on building materials.

ABLACK: I want you to take an interest here. Things could go to
hell if I not here to see after everything myself. Anyhow
what I call you about is the car. You see that car in the lot,
I want it out of there.

CALLISTE *returns to her desk.*

ROOSO: Mr Ablack, you not listening to me. I is the advertiser
for this store in the day. In the night you employ me as a
security. Though I more like a watchman. I tired tell you
give me a gun.

ABLACK: Give you a gun? I must be crazy.

ROOSO: It have bandits around. Rastas forwarding in pairs.
Guerrillas stepping down from the hills, their dreadlocks
hanging, elusive black pimpernels, making getaways like

starboys. Just yesterday they see two of them running away from the burning building across the road. Give me a gun, so maybe I will catch them. I will shoot them down [*he goes down on his belly and takes aim*] like the Flying Squad, like Kojak, like Dick Tracy and Sam Ketchem. I will gun them down, Bz, bz, bz [*rising*]. But you give me a bootoo and a purple uniform, have me masquerading as big sergeant, and I ain't even getting a good constable pay . . . I do it ye-es. I play the part best way I could with a bootoo in my hand. But I don't know how you expect me to shout: Halt! Who goes there? Stop or I'll shoot! or any of the things a real police does have to say. Is like this whole thing is a joke, he! he! And the only reason this store ain't get loot is because people in this area know me. But, I telling you, I don't feel safe.

ABLACK: In the car park, there was a sign, CUSTOMERS ONLY. Where is it?

ROOSO [*feeling put upon*]: I don't like this you know . . . I don't know.

ABLACK: How you will know? But every day you out there. And in the night you's the guard. Rooso, why I can't depend on you? All I want is to be able to depend on you, to – if I turn my back a little – know that it have other eyes that will see . . . [*angrier*] You see that car out there [*a more wicked thought occurs to him*] . . . No. It have two barrels in the back . . .

ROOSO: Mr Ablack, I not working in the back.

ABLACK [*firmly*]: It have two barrels in the back. Roll them out and put them in the parking spot.

ROOSO: Mr Ablack, what is my job?

ABLACK [*with no less firmness*]: It have two barrels in the back . . .

ROOSO *stands confrontationally, angry at the imposition on his dignity.*

ROOSO [*after a pause*]: Mr Ablack, I's a big man. I's a big man, Mr Ablack. I is not a little boy.

ABLACK *says nothing and* ROOSO *marches off as if ignoring the order.*

Halfway across the store, he stops, glares around, fixes his eyes upon
PRIME.

ROOSO [*loud and aggressive*]: Look, next time if you have to call
    me, send somebody else. You see that girl, that girl there!
ABLACK: What's the matter?
ROOSO: That girl, speak to her for me. I . . . I is a big man, you
    hear.
ABLACK [*to* PRIME]: What is this now?
PRIME: He always harassing me, looking at me, telling me
    things, whispering, grumbling, like . . . like he's my father.
ROOSO [*menace in his voice*]: You up and down swizzling your
    little backside, playing you don't know people, playing
    you don't know how to talk to people, playing you better
    than people, playing you ain't have manners. I will teach
    you manners, girl.
PRIME: I don't know what he have with me. I don't know if he
    feel I shouldn't be here. If I not good enough for the store,
    or the store not good enough.
ROOSO: If they didn't teach you manners home, I will teach
    you, girl.
ABLACK [*reprimanding*]: Rooso, what you doing? What is you
    doing?
CALLISTE: Maybe he like her. Everybody round here like her
    [*flashing a look at* ABLACK].
PRIME: Like me? Me? Me? [*superior*]
ROOSO: I can't like you?
PRIME: You better know your place, eh, old man.
ROOSO [*advancing on her, threateningly*]: My place? What is my
    place? What is my place?
PRIME [*fearful, beginning to retreat*]: What you want with me? I
    have done you nothing. I don't know you.
ROOSO [*advancing, menacingly*]: You don't know me? I will make
    you know me, girl.
CALLISTE: Leave her, Rooso! Leave her. She not accustom to
    you.
ABLACK [*sternly*]: Rooso, you have work to do.

ROOSO, *seeing* PRIME *retreat in genuine fear, is surprised and hurt. He stands for a moment with a touching sobriety.*

ROOSO: She fraid me . . . You shouldn't fraid me. I is not the one you should fraid. [*turning to* ABLACK, *his whole tone changed*] What is it you say you want me to do?

ABLACK: Roll out the two barrels. Put them in the parking lot. I don't want anybody park there. Nobody. Let the space stay empty.

ROOSO *exits, hurt, defeated.*

ABLACK [*with self justification looking at the defeated* ROOSO *depart*]: I don't owe him one thing. Waste himself when he was young. Now he want to come and pick and choose what to do. [*he begins to move towards his office, turns to* CALLISTE] Today the world going fast fast fast. Satellites, computers. The jet age. Everybody in the jet age, but we in the donkey cart and [*indicating the departed* ROOSO] mule age. [*he turns back, remembering*] Miss Calliste, you wanted to talk to me?

CALLISTE: Better I see you later, Mr Ablack.

ABLACK: What's wrong with now?

CALLISTE: I don't know if you in the mood. When you in this kinda mood I don't like to talk to you.

ABLACK [*irritated*]: What is it? What is it?

CALLISTE [*resolutely, with an effort*]: Is about my vacation. You say you will let me know today.

ABLACK [*impatient, sharp*]: How much is this vacation now, Miss Calliste?

CALLISTE [*reproachful, decisively*]: Mr Ablack, is seven years I ain't get any vacation at all. And except for that year when the terrible flu pass, the one they call Skylab, I never take sick leave. And when Mr Cherry was here, I didn't take any either.

ABLACK: And you want it now? You didn't take any with Mr Cherry, but with Ablack, you want it.

CALLISTE: I want a rest, a vacation, to go somewhere: Barbados, Grenada.

ABLACK: With your boyfriend? Ah, romance!

CALLISTE: You don't have to make fun of me, Mr Ablack.

ABLACK: Well, how am I to know. You are to age, you know, Miss Calliste. Well, if it is not that urgent, we'll discuss it after we take stock.

CALLISTE: Is years I promising myself a trip. And every year I go to take it, something happen. Year before I had everything book: hotel, plane. And then my mother fall sick.

ABLACK: You'll still have to wait until we take stock.

CALLISTE: I don't know, you know, Mr Ablack. I used to let things go, let what happen happen. Is the will of The Almighty, I used to say. But too many things pass me that way. Now that this leave accumulate, I say I will take a long vacation, go somewhere far where I could maybe meet somebody whose sign correspond with mine, somebody who will care.

ABLACK: Accumulate? How you mean, accumulate?

CALLISTE [*surprised*]: Well, accumulate. Add up. I never take leave under Mr Cherry, so it add up, accumulate.

ABLACK: We have a misunderstanding here. If you earn leave under Cherry, it is Cherry to give it to you. Mr Cherry should have settled with his workers.

CALLISTE: So, Mr Ablack, you mean I have to lose all that leave. Mr Ablack, I can't lose all that leave.

ABLACK: Well, how can I give it? I'm not Cherry. Cherry was the last owner.

As CALLISTE *gazes at* ABLACK *in disbelief, offstage* ROOSO *is heard singing. Dragging a length of chain, he enters singing, as if he is deliberately trying to be a nuisance.*

ROOSO:

       I am a slave
       from a land so far
       I was caught and brought here from Africa.
       I am a slave from a land so far
       I was caught and brought here from Africa.

Well was licks like fire
from the black slave master

[*speaking to himself*] It had black slave masters too, you know.

ABLACK *studiously ignores him. He exits.*

ABLACK [*to* CALLISTE]: You will just have to say, well, it's history. You happened to be here at the wrong time. This is Ablack Hardware Store now. Leave can't accumulate from Cherry . . . And now, now is the time to work, to build. Now is the time to produce, production. Productivity.

CALLISTE: Is easy for you to say that, Mr Ablack. Things change for you, but for me this is the same business, the same store. I doing the same work. I ain't get no promotion, I don't hold no shares . . . Anyway, you wouldn't miss me. You have this girl here. She have her 'A' levels.

ABLACK: Miss Prime is new.

CALLISTE: But I see you training her. Every minute she's in your office. By now she should know everything [*her voice edged with resentment*]. You really don't have no use for me. You don't think so?

ABLACK: Marva, that girl is worrying you?

CALLISTE [*too quickly*]: Me? Worrying me?

ABLACK [*accusingly*]: You know, Miss Calliste, you surprise me. If was one person who I expect to understand the sacrifices we have to make in this store, is you. From the beginning you with us. I don't understand it. You know where we come from, the difficulties we face every day. They don't want us to succeed. Ablack must not succeed. Every day they come with offers to buy me out; they refusing to give me stock; the rumours they spread to keep people suspicious of us . . . What's the matter?

CALLISTE: Mr Ablack, I not comfortable.

ABLACK [*impatiently*]: What you want me to do about the leave?

CALLISTE [*sombrely*]: Is not the leave alone, Mr Ablack. I just

not comfortable. Is like my life just going away here from
me.

ABLACK [*at the end of his patience now*]: Your life? All the time you
didn't know you had a life? When you was working for
Cherry, you didn't have a life? Now, your life! As soon as I
take over: tiredness, vacation life! [*enter* ROOSO *in advertiser's
uniform. He stands as if waiting to speak to* ABLACK. ABLACK
speaks forcefully] You want to speak to me?

ROOSO: I see you talking.

ABLACK *is willing to suspend his conversation with* CALLISTE.

ABLACK: No, you can speak to me now.

ROOSO: I will come back [*he stalks out*].

ABLACK: What I'm saying , Miss Calliste, is that people here
forget responsibility. Nobody thinks about the store.

CALLISTE: You know how I feel Mr Ablack? I feel like I is only a
piece of machine, like the work I doing ain't have nothing
to do with me. Everything is a fuss, the littlest thing, you
make them big big: rules, regulations, sign out for lunch. I
who didn't use to know what name lunch hour. You
watching everything. Everything get near near. Even when
the books correct you have this smile like it ain't true, like
you suspect something. I not comfortable. Something
missing that was here.

ABLACK: So you taking leave to spite me? [*offstage* ROOSO *strikes a
barrel a few ringing blows*] I wonder if Rooso intend to play
the arse with me today.

CALLISTE: Now, I asking myself, Marva, what you putting
yourself out of the way for? Girl, you have leave to take,
take it. You never get to go nowhere, go somewhere. You's
just a worker here. When you dead or sick, they'll get
somebody else: Girls with 'A' levels, young and bright and
pretty . . . Long ago was so different.

ABLACK [*challengingly*]: Under Cherry.

CALLISTE: I talking about when you first take over. So much we
had to do, and though it was only you and me and Rooso,

it was like a family. I didn't use to get tired those days. Now . . .

ABLACK [*sharply*]: Now you ain't have enough to do. People working here forget what work is. Sam with rockers music spending a whole year stacking up a few feet of plywood. Rooso, marching up and down like my store is a blasted stage, grandcharging, bluffing, intimidating people. But I not Cherry. I know him. I know all of you. This is a business. It have to have rules and regulations.

CALLISTE: Rules and regulations?

ABLACK: Yes, rules and regulations. Yes! All about, people ready to say Ablack can't run business, Ablack ain't have the know-how. Laquis have the know-how, but not Ablack. And when I try, when I do something to make this place run proper, my own people complaining. Look at how Rooso behaving! If he intend to keep up his performances, I will fire his arse and forget I did ever know him.

CALLISTE: Mr Ablack, all I want is my vacation, to go Grenada and sit on a beach where nobody don't know me and settle my nerves, and if I meet somebody whose sign correspond with mine, fine; if I don't that will be okay. I ain't even going to look for nobody, cause I know my luck already.

ABLACK: Look at how Rooso behaving! If you waste your life, who's to blame? Life is making use of opportunity; but he want to sing calypso. He want to wear the most tremendous headpiece in the carnival band.

CALLISTE [*to self*]: I am just a worker here.

ABLACK: What you mean? I'm a worker just like you. I work to get this place. I never went on vacation. I never get sick. I never get tired. To get where I is I struggle: I drive taxi, I plant garden. I scheme, I plot, I plan. You feel I inherit this? I struggle for it.

CALLISTE: Why you telling me this, Mr Ablack? It was right here I was working. All the time when this store was Cherry Hardware Store, I was the bookkeeper for Mr Cherry. Before the riots make him run. Dillon get kill in the riots.

ABLACK: I struggle for what I have. Nobody make me a present
of this place.

CALLISTE [*accusingly*]: Mr Ablack, I was the bookkeeper.

ABLACK: Nobody give it to me.

CALLISTE: I used to see things balance. I used to make them
balance. And when Dillon dead, in all those bullets, in all
that noise. When Dillon dead and you get this place, I say,
God make it so. Some must die for some to live. I say,
better you than Cherry. [*pause*] But now . . .

ABLACK [*challengingly*]: Now what, Miss Calliste? What?
[CALLISTE *is silent*] Now what, Miss Calliste?

CALLISTE: I don't know.

ABLACK [*his hurt makes him want to hit back*]: What you don't
know? Miss Calliste, I see is a rat race world. I see that
you have to hustle and scheme and bribe and smile and
bow. All these things I do. What you don't know? But you
balance the books. Why you balance the books? Why?
Why?

CALLISTE: I don't know. Because of a hope . . . that we, a feeling
that after all we go through it had one of us who pull
through . . . Because I did like you.

ABLACK [*resentfully*]: No, you didn't like me. You didn't like me.
You loved Dillon. Dillon the 'revolutionary', the man with
firey words and a dashiki.

CALLISTE: Why I balance the books for you then?

ABLACK: Because I was the bravest of all of you. Because I was
ready to face life as it is, to balance the unbalanced things,
to fight by the rules they fighting, to take my share. Just
like everybody . . . except you.

CALLISTE: I never could take anything for myself, but I did it for
you. I wink at things for you; but for myself, no. I didn't
grow up so.

ABLACK: No. You grow up in the most damn fool way of all the
people in this island. They thief land, they take oil, gravel,
forest, pitchlake, plantation. They never let the law stop
them doing anything. What law? It had no law for them.
You alone more than anybody grow up with the ten

Commandments seasoned in you. And where it put you?
What do you have? Thou shalt not steal, when everybody
else thiefing away the island. And this foolish pride you
have. You don't want to bribe. You can't take a bribe. You
honest. You upright. Well, I grow up so too, Miss Calliste.
But you know what I realize?

CALLISTE [*protesting*]: Well, they teach me wrong.

ABLACK: You know what I realize? I realize that the world
don't sorry for nobody. I realize that I just as bad, just as
terrible as anybody. I could claw too, and sell my brother;
yes, sell his arse! And grab and thief and scheme my way
to the top, wherever they say the top is. Because in this
country, they don't ask to see your heart! They say, show
me your property.

CALLISTE: Let me go on my vacation, Mr Ablack.

ABLACK: You want to run? Where will you go? By the roadside,
stand up at the corner, like a dead zombie, holding up for
people to see a book marked, 'Awake', 'Christ is Coming!'
'The World is Going to end Tomorrow Morning!' Well,
the world is what it is. If you can't deal with it, leave.

CALLISTE: People have to believe in something, Mr Ablack.
People have to have something to believe in.

ABLACK: I believe, Miss Calliste, I believe in the rough and
tumble of this rat-race game. I belive in competition,
survival of the fittest, the weak falling down and the strong
triumphing. [*she looks at him in a kind of horror*] Yes. Start me
at the bottom, I will claw my way to the top. I will not just
survive, I will prevail. [*he pauses, his voice is soft, malicious
almost*] What do you believe in, Miss Calliste?

CALLISTE [*looking at him uncertainly*]: Dillon talked about love,
brotherhood.

ABLACK [*pushing hand in pockets*]: These is my brothers right here
at my side. These is my brothers.

CALLISTE: Dillon died . . . Dillon died.

ABLACK: Dillon was a arse.

CALLISTE: You say that? Yet if it wasn't for Dillon . . . If Dillon
didn't get up, if he didn't rise up, you wouldn't have this
store today.

ABLACK [*insistently*]: Dillon was a arse. Dillon is a guerrilla.
Dillon get shoot down. Miss Calliste, it have ways of doing
things. It have a system. This [*tapping his skull*] is your SLR
and hand grenade. This is your bomb. Out think them,
outsmart them, grind your way to your goal. Put me at the
bottom, I will worm my way to the top.

CALLISTE: Dillon die. You get the store.

ABLACK: If you so believed in Dillon, why you didn't follow him
to the hills? Woman, you didn't go with Dillon, you come
with me. You choose me. Why you left him all alone.
Alone, that's how you left him, you and his wonderful
disciples. You and the people who talk, who demand
heroes. When the time comes for you to stand up with
them, what happens? What happens?

CALLISTE [*wounded*]: Why you tell me this Ashton?

ABLACK: It is time we face facts, Marva. You talk about Dillon
as your great hero, but did you raise a hand to save him?
And, yes, if you so loved Dillon, what the arse you doing
here? [CALLISTE *is speechless*. ABLACK *senses victory and relaxes
into magnanimity*] Every day people come up to me and
shake my hands. They don't even know me. They say,
You's A A Ablack? I say, yes. They say, I just want to tell
you, A A, you going good. If it wasn't for you, we wouldn't
have nobody. Every day they come up to me and shake my
hands and look at the business and say, if it wasn't for you
. . . if it wasn't for me, they wouldn't have one thing in this
island.

CALLISTE [*lifting her head*]: If it wasn't for *you*?

ABLACK: Who else? Rooso, playing the arse, frightening people,
no aim, no object that anybody could see? You, who for
five minutes used to be faithful to every hope that pass
your way, now into your Daily Word and your prayers
and now your vacation. I [*both hands on his breast*] I am the
only one . . . Yes, if it wasn't for *me*. What pride they feel, I
give it to them. [CALLISTE *groans*. ABLACK *is filled with self-
satisfaction*] All I want from my people is to be able to
depend on them. I alone can't make this happen [*his hands
sweep out to indicate the store*]. When people come and say, if

it wasn't for you, I tell them, it's my workers too. You have
your part to play, Miss Calliste. You too, understand that.
But, speak to Rooso. My sympathy is running out. You
can't run a business on sympathy. Speak to him, Miss
Calliste. He is your friend. Speak to him. I am serious . . .
and about your leave, we'll talk about it after stocktaking.

ABLACK *exits*. CALLISTE *sits pensive, takes out her Daily Word, reads.*
PRIME *enters from* ABLACK*'s office, goes to her desk and begins to tidy up
as if to leave.*

PRIME [*after a while*]: Lunchtime, Miss Calliste. [CALLISTE,
    preoccupied with her reading, doesn't look up] What is the word
    today?
CALLISTE: Humble thyself that ye may be exalted.
PRIME: May I go to lunch with you? [CALLISTE *finds this an
    unusual request*] I'll tell you straight. I'm afraid to go out by
    myself. That messenger man, Rooso, he kinda mad? He
    does frighten me. He can't see me pass if he doesn't have
    some stupidness to say. But today is the worst.
CALLISTE: I tell you, he like you.
PRIME: You not serious, Miss Calliste.
CALLISTE: Rooso is not an idiot, you know.
PRIME: Well, if you want to know, that's exactly what he looks
    like to me. One minute he busy busy, next minute he
    making joke, laughing with everybody and then sudden,
    he slow, he grumpy, his nose holes open, his eyes on fire, a
    mad bull, vex with everybody. You going for lunch?
    [CALLISTE *looks at her sharply, restrains herself*] Miss Calliste,
    you all don't like me?
CALLISTE: What you doing for us to like you? You keep your
    smile and politeness for the boss alone. The others of us is
    nothing. You wouldn't even tell Rooso good morning. I
    don't think that you even know Sam working here.
PRIME: I don't like stupid people.
CALLISTE: But they working here with you.
PRIME: So?
CALLISTE: Child, one day you going to learn better.
PRIME: One day you going to learn better. You going to learn

better. Why people always say that to me?

CALLISTE: Oh, other people tell you that too?

PRIME: My father. But he is a sorry person. I see daddy now,
and I remember daddy from those days with the marching
and every minute he going to a meeting. He was in the
revolt, you know.

CALLISTE: Your father was in that? [*more intently concerned*]

PRIME: He used to carry the flags, black, red and green. Every
day he was in the Square. And daddy was tall and his hair
was tall and bushy and he had something in his eyes, a
light, a fire. I remember daddy had this light in his eyes. I
remember that. I was small, so I didn't know what they
was talking about except that it had in it the word black.
And then the marching stop and the flags disappear and
one of daddy friends get shoot.

CALLISTE: Dillon get shoot in that.

PRIME: And daddy quail up like a dried-up governor plum.
Daddy step get light and his voice get hollow and without
no weight, and now, daddy sit down home waiting. I
mean, he working, he moving, but daddy sit down in a
nowhere place, and his hair stop growing. And he should
cut it and let it start to grow again. There was a time when
anything was wrong if daddy had a way to fix it, daddy
had a answer for every problem and his voice had a living
sound, now daddy voice get thin. Daddy not even
criticizing. He just there, and life going.

CALLISTE: Why? What's the reason?

PRIMW: Why I must know why? All I see is the world going on
and people living and I am here now.

CALLISTE: I mean, how you help him?

PRIME: Help him? Daddy should know better. Daddy not a
child. Look, if something is finished, it's finished. You
tried. You had your time. You lose or whatever, it's over,
and you go on. But daddy won't go on.

CALLISTE: Sometimes you can't go on. You don't know where
to go. You only had that one vision, and it was all you had
to guide you; and when it's gone, it leaves you in a
nowhere place.

PRIME [*surprised and delighted at her perception*]: That's exactly where daddy is, nowhere. That's where everybody is, except Mr Ablack. You feel I don't like people. But Rooso is nowhere and Sam, with his music and his ganja – nowhere.

CALLISTE: And me?

PRIME: You? [*she smiles*] You have your Daily Word.

CALLISTE: You should try to understand people. People trying.

PRIME: Trying. You call sitting down trying?

CALLISTE: Rooso sitting down too?

PRIME: No. Rooso crazy. One minute he busy busy. Next time he slow and sullen and grumpy. Then he laugh and then he vex with everybody..

CALLISTE: People think Rooso crazy. But sometimes I does see in his eyes a fire. I does see a vexation take him over and then he does hold himself in check, and go back to be the clown. But one day he going to get up. I know it. Maybe your father is like that too.

PRIME: No. The fire gone from daddy. Daddy dead.

CALLISTE: Look Celia. Celia is your name, not so? Take your time to judge. Take your time to make up your mind so that when you finish choose you won't be sorry. Don't be too hurry. I make that mistake already.

PRIME [*feeling a closeness with* CALLISTE]: You know today is the first day I really talk to you.

CALLISTE: Okay, I'll go to lunch with you. But Rooso not going to harm you. Look, after we finish eat, let's pass by the corner and hear him sing. You'll see what I mean.

PRIME: Who? Rooso? Sing?

CALLISTE: You didn't know he is a calypsonian? Every lunch hour he does be at the corner at that empty spot that used to be a rum shop that burn down. A whole crowd does be there. You never hear him?

PRIME: Oh, he's the one. Once. But Miss Calliste, it's terrible. People around watching him, asking him, Rooso, give we a calypso, mamaguying him, laughing at him. Their faces grinning, and he in the midst of them, somebody for them to feel superior to. Terrible.

CALLISTE: And without him, what they have?

PRIME: But it's terrible. He should stop it. I mean, all that embarrassment. All those stupid people. And he singing stupidness too. [ROOSO *has entered softly and is near enough to overhear without being seen. He's in his security uniform*] They laugh at him that ugly laughter. And you know he is dying to sing another tune. They don't hear it, whatever it is he trying to say. [*she spots him*] Oh gosh! Look him!

ROOSO *walks forward singing 'Trinidad and Tobago' song (see Sparrow).*

CALLISTE: Rooso, you not singing today? We was just coming to hear you.

ROOSO: You feel I don't know people laugh at me. I amuse them. I amuse the fools.

CALLISTE: They laugh, but you know they don't mean nothing. If they laugh is because they don't know what else to do. They embarrassed.

ROOSO: I carry their embarrassment. I carry it . . . [*pause*] You know I don't even know if people really want me to sing, if they really want to hear what I have to say . . . I need to stop singing, you know. Ban myself. Take a rest. [*to audience*] All you will like that, eh? You will say, at last we catch Rooso. We retire him. We park up the arse. [*to CALLISTE*] You know they wouldn't even say that. That is how much they care. [*to audience*] One of these days I will get tired, I will just break away, I will just disappear into nowhere, miraculous, like a long line of smoke that was never there; and some time long long after, maybe when you get old, or when something happen in your life that bring you back to this spot and this time, you will say . . . you will say: You know it had a fella used to sing calypso here name . . . and you wouldn't even remember my name was Rooso; and you wouldn't even know what emptiness my absence leave you in. You wouldn't even know. [*to CALLISTE*] If Ablack ask for me tell him I gone to lunch [*he turns to exit*].

CALLISTE *and* PRIME *are about to leave and they all begin to exit when*
ABLACK *emerges from his office.* ABLACK *claps his hands.*

ABLACK : Hello, hello, hello. What the arse is this, Rooso? This
is a new style or what? Since when you does wear your
security uniform in the day? [ROOSO *halts, dignified*] That
uniform is for the night. [ROOSO *stands firm,* ABLACK, *at the
end of his patience, addresses the ladies*] Ladies, I want you to
come into my office and look through the window and into
the parking lot and tell me what you see. Come! [*to* ROOSO]
You wait here! [ABLACK *and ladies exit into* ABLACK *'s office.*
ROOSO *straightens up his uniform*] Yes, the car still there.
[ABLACK *and ladies return.* ABLACK *speaks angrily*] Rooso, you
know it have a car in the parking lot.

ROOSO : If you see one, it there yes.

ABLACK : And where the barrels that I ask you to roll out?

ROOSO : Where the barrels does always be. In the back . . . Mr
Ablack, you want me to push barrels in this uniform? You
ever see a police pushing barrel?

ABLACK : Then why you change your clothes?

ROOSO : So I could be official. So I could go and talk to the
driver that park in your lot. If I have to act as security, I
must have on my security clothes. I must be official.

ABLACK [*to Ladies*] : You see the nonsense I am talking about?
You see it!

ROOSO [*dignified*] : Mr Ablack, I don't like how you does talk to
me [*he begins to move off purposefully but without hurry*].

ABLACK : Where are you going? I talking to you, man.

ROOSO [*with restraint and dignity*] : Mr Ablack, now is my lunch
hour. I have people waiting on me. They come from all
parts: Barataria, San Juan, Diego Martin, Laventille. Is
only their lunch hour they could spare from the work they
doing. They don't have time to wait. I is the only one they
have to cheer them up, to give them something, to lighten
the burden of their life a little; so that after they hear me
and they go back to work, they still smiling, they still
thinking, Gosh, we living. They don't get that on TV or
where they working. I alone give them something.

ABLACK: You see today, Rooso. Today I in a evil mood.
    However you do it, whatever you do, I want those barrels
    inside that parking lot and the car out of there before you
    leave. Your singing is your business.

CALLISTE: But he could do it when he come back.

ABLACK: I don't want to hear you, Miss Calliste. I am tired. If
    he want to go and sing, let him tender his resignation. My
    work have to go on. [ROOSO *shrugs, slips into a lackadaisical
    attitude as if on the way to the unpleasant task. He stops. Disgust
    overwhelms him. He rushes off stage.* ABLACK *speaks angrily*] You
    have to keep behind him, rough him up to get him to do
    anything. [*from offstage we hear barrels tumbling, then with a
    bang they stop. Enter* ROOSO *with the speed of his vexation. Over
    his security uniform is his clown suit, with the placards. He goes
    directly to* ABLACK] Now, what is this now?

ROOSO: I resign.

ABLACK *tries to look amused. Actors freeze as curtain is drawn.*

Act Two

Lights up on the hardware store. Actors unfreeze.

ABLACK : You resign? [*trying to look amused*]

ROOSO [*taking off the placards and handing them to* ABLACK]: These is your placards. These is your placards with the announcements that I make for you in front this store for ten years. I do it good. [ABLACK *refuses to accept placards.* ROOSO *throws them to the ground*] And these [*ripping off the stripes on the shoulders of his uniform*]. These is the three stripes that you make me a sergeant with, though you give me less than a real constable pay. I must look the part, you say. But you wouldn't pay for it [*pulls off stripe*]. You wouldn't pay. [*pulls more roughly*]

ABLACK [*with performed alarm*]: Watch how you pulling off them stripes, eh! You will tear that uniform. Last time you do this foolishness I had was to buy a new shirt. These things cost money . . . When you leave here, where you will go? [ROOSO *pulls off stripes more roughly and dashes them to the floor.* ABLACK *'s anger is mixed with amusement*] Rooso, don't play the arse, you hear. I tired with you and these performances. They disrupt my work, encourage indiscipline and set a bad example for the rest of the staff.

ROOSO [*taking off cap*]: This is your cap. [*flings cap across the room*]

ABLACK [*patiently*]: Miss Prime, take up that cap for me, please.

ROOSO *steps backwards, draws the baton from his pocket and holds it upraised over* ABLACK *(as if to strike him) while* ABLACK *is turned to* PRIME.

CALLISTE [*alarmed, rushes forward to restrain* ROOSO, *screams*]: Rooso! What you doing? You'll get yourself in trouble.

ABLACK [*seeing the danger*]: Don't worry with him. One of these days he going to go too far. You think he crazy to hit me.

ROOSO *brings the baton down and points it, thrusts it really, at* ABLACK .

ROOSO : And this is your bootoo, the rod of protection that I
    protect this whole place with, because you never give me a
    gun. I tired ask you for a gun, but you never give me a gun.
    I suppose I was no real police anyway. And this whole
    thing is a masquerade, a play, like 'As You Like It' or
    Derek Walcott.

He pushes the baton at ABLACK. ABLACK *takes it.*

ABLACK : Yes, you better give me that.

ROOSO *takes off his boots, kicking them off his feet, rips open his shirt.*
PRIME *moves as if to take up the boots.*

ROOSO : You [*to* PRIME], don't touch those boots! Don't touch
    them. That is not your work.

PRIME *freezes.*

ABLACK [*watchful as* ROOSO *rips open shirt*]: Man . . . Man, what
    the arse wrong with you? Don't play the fool and take off
    your clothes and expose yourself here, you know. What
    wrong with you?
ROOSO : Mr Ablack, I's a big man, you hear.
ABLACK : What you so touchous about? So nobody can't talk to
    you, eh? eh? All I want is to be able to depend on you. Mr
    Cherry depend on you. Wonderfully, you protect his
    property. You wasn't even a watchman on his place. You
    was a handyman. But nobody couldn't stand up two
    minutes round this store when you was near. Cherry, the
    whiteman, depend on you and you never let him down.
    But me, I can't talk to you.
ROOSO : With Mr Cherry it was different.
ABLACK [*heatedly*]: Of course it was different. *I* pay you to
    advertise. *I* give you a uniform and a baton to keep
    security. You do that free for Cherry. I put three stripes on
    your shoulders . . .
ROOSO : Three stripes, and what pay?

ABLACK: Three stripes to give you a sense of your dignity.

ROOSO: But you not dealing with my dignity.

ABLACK: You think even in a joke, you coulda be a sergeant with Cherry?

ROOSO: With Mr Cherry it was different. We had a understanding. I battling him, and he battling me. We wasn't friends.

ABLACK: And since *we* is friends, since we start out together working for Cherry, I is your enemy? Ain't I is your enemy?

ROOSO: I didn't say that, you know. I didn't say that.

ABLACK: Well, what you mean? You say that you and Cherry wasn't friends. Well, what I is to you? Tell me! What you mean [*aggressively*]

ROOSO [*defensively*]: You hear you! You always trying to make me feel like I is some kinda traitor, like I owe you some special something. Well, I don't owe you. I don't owe you.

ABLACK: But is you who say we is friends.

ROOSO: I battling for my life, Mr Ablack.

ABLACK: Hear the word: Life! The new word in the lexicon of black dictionary.

ROOSO: You know you all don't know people. Same thing with Mr Cherry. He watch me, see me looking hungry. He know I in need, cause is he paying me the next-to-nothing salary. He want me to thief. He dying for me to thief. Leaving his wallet lying around, leaving the drawer open with money, leaving me to close up the store; and all around is everything: galvanize, boards, hinges, nails, [*proudly*] I never put a nail in my pocket. I was living in a shack and I never put a nail in my pocket.

ABLACK [*excitedly*]: You see! You see! You wanted to show Cherry that you was honest. Cherry take you for a damn thief, so you wanted to show him you was honest. What you want to show me? What? *What you want to show me?* That you could take off your clothes and expose yourself in my store? Cherry coulda close his eyes and leave you here and you'd see everything run proper; but me! Why I can't depend on you? Why?

ROOSO [*almost with sorrow at* ABLACK's *denseness*]: But how *you*
could depend on *me*, Mr Ablack? How *you* could depend on
me? [*pause*] You not listening to what I tell you. You not
listening. My whole life I fighting for my life, to use this
freedom to be free, to pause, to breathe, to be, to stop
going going going like a blasted wind-up machine, going
at a crazy speed for somebody profit. How you could
depend on me? Is my life I fighting for.

ABLACK: You fighting for what life? [*to* CALLISTE *and* PRIME] You
hear him? He fighting for his life. Lie! Is not that at all.
Envy. Disrespect. Black people! He fighting me. I ain't
good enough.

ROOSO [*feeling the need to defend this accusation*]: It ain't that.

ABLACK [*heatedly pressing his point home*]: Yes, is that. What else?
You don't really like to work for me . . . You think I don't
deserve a store? A sign? Somebody to advertise me to the
world? To say A A Ablack Hardware store? A A Ablack
Hardware Store for a blasted change! You don't think is
time we say, A A Ablack Hardware Store for a blasted
change? AA!

ROOSO [*sincerely*]: I don't want to battle you, Mr Ablack.

ABLACK [*almost with matching sincerity*]: Well, is better you battle
me, Rooso. Battle me! Cause it ain't fair, you hear. It
damn well not fair for my own people to come and deny
me my success. I paid the price, man. I went down on my
belly. I beg, I scheme, I thief, and I arrive.

ROOSO [*outraged*]: So because you beg and scheme and thief
that qualify you? That is your certificate? Because you beg
and scheme and thief?

ABLACK [*looking at the women*]: You see! You see! I just say, thief,
and hear how he catch at it. [*to* ROOSO] Hear you! You
glad to hear I thief. You jump at it like you's the AG. Well,
lock me up. Look the telephone there. Call the police. Call
them. Go ahead. See if you know a police I don't know. Go
on. Go on. [*pause*] Yes, I organize myself. I do what I had
to do. But you think is me alone? You know is not me
alone. But, you know what the other people woulda do, if I
was one of them? They would congratulate me, hold a

feast, kill a goat, put me on the throne. But, we? You looking cokey eye at me.

ROOSO [*to the women*]: You hear how he twist up what I say?

ABLACK: But I understand you. I understand you, Rooso. Is because you have no ambition, nowhere to go, you must strive to keep everybody at your level. Look, we come in town together, you and me. What you do? What you do with your [*pause*] life? [ROOSO *begins to take off his shirt*] Yes, take it off! Take it off! Get vex! That is how you answer facts. Get vex. That's all you could do. But I talking the truth. You don't have one thing to show for your years. You didn't work. You didn't sacrifice. Fete is all you know. Fete!

ROOSO: You mean that that is all you see from me? For all these years you so close to me, that is all you see from me?

ABLACK: Well, what else to see? What else you show me? And that you was strong. You one coulda tote two bags of rice on your shoulders.

ROOSO: Yes.

ABLACK: Yes what?

ROOSO: Yes, I come in town young, strong, full with my rhythm [*he begins to move almost lyrically*]. I sing calypso, I beat steelband. I play the Glory of Greece, The Fall of Babylon. I dance. My headpiece was the whole island. I had no wheels to ease the strain. I carry, me one – carry everybody on these shoulders [*stretching out his arms like he's carrying a headpiece*]. I dance, holding them up like gems, the sequins and rhinestones in the crown of my shining headpiece. I dance from Jour Ouvert morning till last lap Tuesday. [*chanting*] All Stars! All Stars! Despers! Despers!

Accompanying music of Jour Ouvert morning. Crowd chanting: All Stars! All Stars!

ABLACK [*stepping forward with the movements of a midnight robber*]: I was in that band.

ROOSO [*miming dance with headpiece on shoulders*]: I show the steps of freedom. I was fertility, I was love. Spectators looking

on, marvelling as I balance on my shoulders the giant
hosay of these islands. I say, Come in . . .

CALLISTE *and* PRIME *begin to dance as they enter the band.*

ABLACK [*still as midnight robber*]: I had my own rhythm. A off-
key, simi-dimi kind of ratchefy . . .
ROOSO: I say, come in. Come in . . .

CALLISTE *and* PRIME *dance separately,* CALLISTE *as one familiar with
the music,* PRIME *awkwardly as a visitor.*

ABLACK [*as robber*]: From the far lands. From the far far
badlands of New Mexico, Arizona, Tuscan. I, King Get
Truer, hat tall, flowing cape, pistol and dagger, robust
man, choke and robber, enter the arena, crying, the last
shall be first and the first last. Gimme piece of the action
too. I, the bandit son of the the Unknown Bandit, declare,
I come to claim my share of the loot.

Jour Ouvert morning music continues.

ROOSO [*still dancing. To* PRIME *and* CALLISTE]: Let me show you
the steps.

PRIME *is unfamiliar with music, but trying to get into rhythm.*

ABLACK [*whirling upon* PRIME]: No. No. Not so fair maiden, for
while you may look innocent like snow, the crimes you
have committed will take up pages and pages of the desert
lands of the Sahara, will cover the mountains of Mexico
and Peru. My dagger is ready to drip blood. Blood for the
remission of your sins, before you enter.

PRIME *shrinks back and* ROOSO *comes to her rescue, holds her around her
waist. They dance, she, uncomfortably, out of step.*

ROOSO : Let me show you the steps [*shows her as* ABLACK *turns to audience*].

ABLACK : At my birth the sun didn't shine. The stars all withdrew far into the depths of the Universe, so dismal was my shadow; for I was the most most notorious, most criminal bandit, grandmaster born upon the earth. In the deadly stillness of that midnight morning of my birth, I heard a voice crying down from the distance of ages, My son, my son, go forward with your pistol and dagger, your poisons, bombs and dynamite, kill for the sake of killing, let the world know the beauty of evil, take treasure from the poor and give to the rich. Let the rich gather up rubies, emeralds, diamonds and various precious stones and hand them over to their children in every generation, so that evil will live on. So, to fulfil the wishes of my father, the grandest, most notorious criminal who has no name, I will slay, kill and devour, unless you empty your treasures and give them to me. [*he blows his whistle*. PRIME, *who has been uncomfortable with* ROOSO *all along, now slips out of embrace*. ABLACK *sees this and laughs*] Ha! ha! ha! You don't see she don't want to jump up with you!

CALLISTE : Why you don't jump up with me?

ABLACK : Do like them. Stick to your own.

ROOSO *stands uncomfortably* (*music has stopped*).

ABLACK [*mocking*] : Is friends you want? Let me hear your song now. Sing it! Sing it!

ROOSO [*arms outflung, chants*] : All Stars! All Stars! All Stars! All Stars!

ABLACK : Sing the song that you win the crown with. Sing, let me hear. [*singing ironically*]

> The Negro, the Indian, the Whiteman, the Chiney
> live as one family
> In this wonderland of Calypso
> In this wonderland of steelband
> Where I was born . . . [*speaking*] Sing it!

ROOSO [*chanting*]: All Stars! All Stars!

ABLACK: Sing it.

ROOSO [*with conviction*]: Yes, I sing that song. [*all look at him*]

ABLACK: You must sing it. You want friends. You can't stand
on your own two feet, you see. You can't stand alone.

CALLISTE: Why is you alone singing that song? And is you who
beat the drum, why you have to dance it too? Why nobody
not coming in and helping you with the chorus? Why you?

ABLACK [*overbearing*]: I could stand up for myself. Alone! I don't
want no damn friends. I know myself. I know my history. I
was Pharaoh in the Cushite dynasty, I was Amazons at the
court of the King of Dahomey, I was prince of Ghana,
doctor of Timbuktu, warrior of Ashanti, merchant from
the Limpopo to the Zambezi.

CALLISTE [*gently to* ROOSO]: Why you?

ROOSO [*fumbly, defensively*]: You see, I know the words. Is I
make up the tune.

CALLISTE: Yes.

ROOSO: You see, is a kinda experience you go through.
[CALLISTE *and* ABLACK *look at him unconvinced*] A holiness that
come out of crucifixion and the glory of rising. [*louder*] I
understand suffering. [*trying to be convincing*] I am not afraid
of people. This is a new world, a new chance. The universe
is here. It belongs to all people. We each must become
everybody.

CALLISTE: But you alone? You alone could make it true?

ABLACK [*cynically*]: You alone know music? You alone could
dance? What the arse wrong with you? You alone could
dance up a nation from these scraps of confusion, while
everybody else grabbing for theirself? Watch what I doing.
[*as midnight robber*] From the far lands. From the far far
badlands, I cry. Piece of the action too. And look, your
woman. Look, your children. Look at their condition.

CALLISTE: Why don't you sing a song for me.

PRIME [*as child*]: Sing a song for us, daddy. Mammy tired from
ironing, the radio not playing. When we going to get a
TV?

ROOSO: For you? For you alone?

CALLISTE: All the tenderness and consideration you lavish on other people, and you don't have no song for me? On the neighbour radio, and on her TV, I hear other people singing soft songs of love. I see them making their women queens. [ROOSO *goes to speak*] And don't tell me I is a queen already.

ROOSO: I have to find the words. I have to change the language. I . . . I trying.

ABLACK: Why you don't sing, 'Baby, it's cold outside. Come close to me'. That is a nice one.

ROOSO [*to* CALLISTE]: I trying . . . But my words drift off into a joke, into protest.

ABLACK [*punishing*]: Dingolay, breakaway, bamsie, bumbulum. That is how you celebrate your woman. Jam! Jam! Jam!

PRIME [*as child*]: Daddy, I want to be a star on the screen. On TV

ABLACK: Ha! Ha! Which TV? What screen? What star? A mon-star? Hahaha!

PRIME: I want to be a model.

ABLACK: To model what? Black pepper? Pots and pans? The model of toilet paper and soap powder. That is all they will let you advertise unless you have the money. Don't you read? Don't you see? [*to* ROOSO] Sing the song. Sing how the Negro, the Indian, the Whiteman, the Chiney live as one happy family, only because the Negro so stupidee. Sing it.

ROOSO: I come in town young, full with my rhythm. I play the Glory of Greece, The Fall of Babylon. My headpiece was the whole island, people, the gleaming rhinestones and sequins in the crown of my headpiece. I say, Come in and dance, I will show you the steps. Come in and sing, I will teach you the song . . .

ABLACK [*singing*]: But when Carnival come and pass [*he breaks off*]. You have a better voice than me. Sing it.

ROOSO: That doesn't stop me.

ABLACK: Sing it, let everybody hear.

ROOSO [*singing, almost sadly*]:
Carnival is such a beautiful scenery
Carnival is a gift from the Almighty
Of all the places of the world, in Trinidad you'll see
How all the races does join as one family.

ABLACK [*shouting in vexation*]: Sing it.

ROOSO:

But when Carnival come and pass
People does go back to their race and class
So the only thing to keep us together is mas!

[*Repeat.* ROOSO *deeply emotional*] Mas! Mas! Mas in yuh arse! [*he stands proudly*] I come in town young, full with my rhythm. I didn't chinks. I stand my hand like a man. My headpiece was the whole island. I had no wheels to ease the strain. I had no wings to fly. I bear everybody, me one on these shoulders. I dance for freedom. I dance for love. I call everybody inside the band: Come in! You could dream to imagine my ambition? Your store, your money. Brother, that is not the scene I on.

Silence.

ABLACK [*applauding*]: Three cheers for Rooso! Hip! Hip! Hip! Hip! Hip! Hip! [*to audience*] All you not applauding? You not giving him a hand? This is the Great Sacrificer, feting all his life, looking to hold up people woman in the band. Here is the new world man, longing for people to have dignity, coming after Daaga, Cuffie, Makandal, Dessalines, the Tiger, coming after the Middle Passage and sugar cane plantations to say love. Bringing out his calypso, tuning his pan, making his carnival a ceremony each year to join people to people. And the arse ain't have a cent in his pocket. [*to* ROOSO] Every year you fulling up Port of Spain with bands, your music ringing, your headpiece dazzling, and what you have? What do you have, jackass? All ah we is one? That is your great ambition? [*draws himself up to a full firmness, with contempt*

almost] Now, will you please gather the pieces of your
uniform and get back to work, since is here you working,
and this store have to be protected from your more
ferocious brethren. Singing and dancing don't count.
Money, brother. Money. We need the money. [*laughs*]

ROOSO: I stand my hand. I didn't chinks. I didn't hide. I
forward myself like a man. I stand up for every freedom in
this island. I march for Young Power, Black Power, Power
to the People. I was in front every rebellion.

ABLACK [*as an aside*]: You don't know, jackass, that in this
place, you's the only one does think bout freedom.
[*parodying, as he punches one clenched fist in the air*] Power to the
People! Black Power! Black Beauty! Black Mathematics!
Black English! Black Love! Brothers and Sisters, you
listen but you do not hear, you see but do not grasp. The
white world has not deceived, you, it is you who have
deceived yourself. You continue to believe that white is
white, that the whiteness of white is the whiteness of
purity. Listen to the heroes of the white world: Cortes,
Pizzaro, Balboa, Frankenstein, Jesse James, Bonnie and
Clyde, Jack the Ripper. This is no laughing matter. They
have written them down in their histories. They have
celebrated them in movies and comic books: Cesar Borgia,
Al Capone alias Scarface, Sir Francis Drake, Sir John
Hawkins, Beelzebub, Baby Face Nelson, The Dalton
Brothers, Columbus . . .

ROOSO: I marched all over the town for freedom, while you . . .

ABLACK: While I, yes, was counting the money I saved up to see
if I could take over the business that Cherry was running
from. You think I didn't see what was happening, which
kind of people was marching? You think I didn't realize
that when we stop marching we would just be more tired
people with the same nothing. Go on. Go on.

ROOSO: You get the business, I get put in jail. When I come
out, you give me a job.

ABLACK: Brains, Rooso. I tell you, this [*tapping his skull*] is your
SLR and hand grenade. You must know how to stoop to
conquer. There is a time, fella, when you have to say,

Enough. Enough. Let me stop here and see what I want.
But how can you answer that question when you don't
know what you want, when, for you, rebellion is just a
habit. I mean, can you tell me what you want? Tell me!

ROOSO [*reflectively*]: I run to the hills. I get shoot down. [*to*
CALLISTE] And all the time going over in my brain is the
song I trying to sing: Baby, baa-by, you're too fine to live
this way.

ABLACK: Well, you marched, okay. Okay. You did something.
Cherry and some of them run. But, admit it. Admit it. All
you was just a set of arses marching up and down the
country, while property was up for sale. Admit it!

ROOSO: Baaa-by. Baby, you're too fine to live this way.

ABLACK: Where are the marchers now? Where them?

ROOSO: Nowhere. The marchers ain't nowhere. You are
somewhere, no so? We marched for you. That satisfy you?
[*he moves menacingly towards* ABLACK] You feel I march to put
you where you is?

CALLISTE [*seeking to calm him*]: Rooso! Rooso!

ROOSO: Where you is? You feel the world really run by guess?
That success is a chance, a number that pop up on the
spinning wheel of a lottery, just so without no sweat. Just
so, without no sweat?

CALLISTE [*touching his arm also to divert him*]: Baby? You called
me baby?

ROOSO: I wanted to sing, baby; but every time I go to fill in the
words, you was gone.

CALLISTE: I . . . I waited a long time.

ROOSO [*sadly*]: I wish you did wait a little longer. I know you
did already wait too long, and that you had to look for
shelter, you had to find somewhere safe for you and the
child to lie down. But I . . . I had was to be on the move. I
had to dance. I had to dance the stickman dance. I had to
go down low, kick out my feet in a Bongo and slide off in
my Fireman, then rise up to chip slow, making the cool
long moves of the King Sailor, shaking my head soft so I
wouldn't overbalance the headpiece that I was bearing so
long. It takes time.

CALLISTE: I really didn't mean to run. But was a long time you was gone. And I didn't get no letter. The rumour was that you was in Venezuela. People say they see you on the wharf trying to get a boat to go America.

ROOSO: And you believed them? You believe that I would take of just so and go?

CALLISTE [*regretfully*]: I didn't know. I had to do something . . . And then I meet this fella I used to know.

ROOSO [*with concern*]: Look at your hair! What you do with your hair?

CALLISTE: I had to get in fashion, to be one of everybody, so they wouldn't be able to single me out for persecution. For black was no longer in. All them fellows who used to be in the marching throw off their dashiki. For a while they was in shirtjacks, then they went back to three-piece suit.

ROOSO: In the hot sun?

CALLISTE: In the same sun.

ROOSO [*moving to embrace her*]: Oh, woman!

ABLACK: Okay, hero. Where are you now?

ROOSO [*staring off into space*]: I'm in the hills . . . with the pipes of frogs and the hooting of owls and the peace of hushing trees. Me one.

CALLISTE [*narrator-like*]: Pausing after the long march.

PRIME [*also narrator*]: Resting in the shade of angelin trees.

ROOSO *mimes*.

CALLISTE: His sigh is louder than the wind. He rises, goes to the stream. He drinks, washes his face, drinks again and watches the swiftly flowing crystal of the sun swim away in fragments, and his life swim away, his time swim away. He is thinking, 'how old is this river? how old is this world?'

PRIME: A great grey chicken hawk plunges out of the sky, bringing the panic cries of small birds. A twig snaps. Awake, he quivers like a wild animal. He goes to run. He wants to run. But his feet are roots of a mahogany tree.

ABLACK [*like a hunter, pointing a gun at* ROOSO]: You bitch, we

catch you. You are surrounded [*talking as through a
megaphone*]. Throw down your weapons and put up your
hands. [ROOSO *puts his hands up.* ABLACK *speaks harshly, as he
moves forward out of the shadows*] Throw down your weapons!
I order you.

ROOSO: But chief, my hands are empty.

ABLACK: Don't talk back. Throw down your weapons.

ROOSO: But, chief, my weapons is me, a heart that feels and
eyes that see.

ABLACK [*insistently*]: I don't want all that smart talk. For the last
time, throw down your weapons! You playing the arse,
saying you's a guerrilla, have me out here in this bush
when I could be home with my woman. Say your prayers.

ROOSO: Before you shoot me, tell me, what is my crime? You
have to have a warrant with my crime.

ABLACK: A warrant with his crime! You hear him! Like a
blasted lawyer, like if out here in the bush I have to give
him any explanation. [*he goes closer to* ROOSO *and holds up the
gun*] Here I am . . . this gun is defence, prosecutor, judge
and executioner; but you want a warrant with your crime.
[*turning upon him and shouting*] You think you commit one
crime?

ROOSO [*a bit shaky*]: My crimes, then.

ABLACK: For resisting our new world of colour television,
refrigerators, the shift system and the Point Lisas
industrial promise. For insisting that you have a life. For
suggesting that you are capable of creating on your own. I
tell you, we have to rely on overseas experts.

PRIME [*seated now at table, is an announcer on radio programme. Her
voice soft, lulling*]: Overseas experts will create a paradise
for you. They are being brought in from all corners of the
globe. With their magic wands, they will build your roads,
construct your houses, repair your telephones,
manufacture your stereos so that you can get your disco
music. Your water system will be run by them, your
sewerage bowls. You will have nothing to do.

ABLACK: Why don't you understand?

ROOSO: But I ain't doing you nothing. I living my own life.

ABLACK [*furiously*]: You own life? [*strikes him*] You keep insisting that you have a life. Why are you making trouble? Who is paying you? Why are you doubting the paradise that I am creating? You fool, do you want to try to do things for yourself and make a mess of them? I tell you, we will import a life for you, and assemble it locally.

ROOSO [*frightened, but courageous*]: Don't we have our own history? We have nothing new to bring into the world? because of our suffering? our unique prevailing? our crucifixion, our rising? We have no history of our own to begin?

ABLACK [*furious with exasperation*]: There is only one history.

PRIME [*announcing*]: There is only one history. One history. Columbus began it. Black enslavement and Indian indenture, Chinese indenture, White indenture, for as you know, criminal elements of the Whites were also indentured, and the Portuguese. These brought us into the mainstream of the modern world. Now we can get to make trips to see England, the United States. Today a number of our citizens do their shopping in Miami and jet back home. This is called jet-setting. And we return with all sorts of items, because, as you know, we have created nothing, we come from no where: we are here simply to learn. As one great writer put it: We are the students of the world.

ABLACK [*furious and all-powerful*]: Get that into your skull. Why are you making trouble? Don't you know that I am tired of shooting you down, jailing you, lynching you, starving you? Don't you know that I am tired? I had to whip you on the plantations. I had to put down your rebellions. I give you a constitution that I bring in from England, you wouldn't settle down. What the hell you want?

ROOSO: Who . . . who are you? What are you protecting? What do you stand for? Who are you? [*genuinely afraid for the first time*] Who are you?

ABLACK [*a devilish laugh*]: Don't you know who I am? [*in a loud voice*] I tell you to throw down your weapons. You are forcing me to fire! He is trying to escape. Look out for his

razor! Take cover, men. You are forcing me to shoot.
[*shoots*]

ROOSO *holds his groin and with a grimace of pain, very theatrically,
begins to fall.*

ROOSO [*in pain*]: You win, Mr Ablack. You win . . . goodbye
world. Goodbye Trinidad and Tobago. Goodbye Invaders
Steelband on J'ouvert morning, and Despers and All Stars
at Panorama. Keep up the good work Stalin. Sing
Valentino. Blow their mind Shadow. Stay up
Zimbabwe . . . stay up Auntie Kay. Stay up Kojak. Keep
Trinidad clean. Keep the city clean . . . Oh Lord, I dying
in truth, I dying. [*chanting*] All Stars! All Stars! Despers!
Despers! Goodbye Laventille. Laventille, goodbye. [*with
urgency*] All the newspapers and magazines. All the
historians and commentators. Remember me when you
writing your books. Remember Rooso who used to sing by
the burn down corner where Black Cat Bar used to be.
Remember me, Rooso [*spelling*] R-O-O-S-O. Don't forget
the name. And that woman, my woman, I wish I had been
around to warm you with the pittance of my love . . . Duty.
You expected from me duty, and you did not know that
my highest duty is my love. And the song you asked me
about. The song. I thought my life would be that song,
that song, my life . . . I . . . I die.

ROOSO *slumps to the ground. The women move forward with mournful
cries,* ABLACK *also steps forward.*

ABLACK [*commandeering the situation*]: Stand back! Stand back!
Get him into the van. [*the bereaved women move aside.* ABLACK
fixes his clothes and faces reporters from the media] We got a tip off
that they were hiding in the bush. We approached their
hideout and surrounded the area. At exactly six hours we
moved in. They opened fire. We returned their fire. When
it was over, one lay dead. We want the public to know that

these are dangerous criminals. In their hideout was one of the biggest caches of dangerous weapons found to date in the island: one automatic Afro comb [*he produces the item*], two sticks of dynamite marijuana [*item*], a recoiling slingshot. One copy of Slavery to Capitalism. One copy of From Columbus to Castro . . . Castro, take note. We are not dismissing the possibility that the Cubans may be involved. We have notified next of kin, but nobody has come forward to claim the body of the dead.

ROOSO [*jumping to his feet*]: But, you lie. I ain't dead at all. The world is not a stage, Mr Ablack. It is real. My life is real.

ABLACK: Good. So will you please get your arse back to work, or, you still resign?

ROOSO: The world don't run by guess, Mr Ablack. We can't build a world by trickery, by bribery, by scheme. We can't build a world with people that create nothing, exploit people, rip off everything. We can't build a world that rewards the smartman and calls the honest man a fool. You laugh at the word 'honest'. Yes. That is where we reach, honest ain't even something you could say. How could you believe that after all I go through, that now after I survive, after I come through, that all I interested in is just money, money. I want the money, money.

CALLISTE [*with surprise*]: It's Dillon. [*she moves towards* ROOSO] Dillon!

ROOSO: Marva!

CALLISTE [*her gladness mitigated by feelings of guilt*]: But I thought . . . it was on the radio, . . . You didn't die? They didn't shoot you?

ROOSO [*confidently*]: Shit cannot defeat me. You know that. Come, let's go. We have life to live and work to do.

CALLISTE: I have something to tell you. [*her tone alerting him of something, he is now a little uncertain, looks at her suspectingly*]

ROOSO: I know, it musta been hard on you . . . You and? [*he looks at* ABLACK. *He looks back at her. They look at each other in silence as if trying to figure out what has changed in the other*]

CALLISTE [*calmly, courageously*]: I denied you. I didn't claim you. I ran away. I am a traitor. When I saw them throw your

body into the van, it suddenly came to me. What is the
sense of all this? This struggling for justice and honour?
What is the use of trying to make things better? Will
things ever get better? And the people? The people? They
don't help you.

ROOSO: They can't do better. They don't know their power.

CALLISTE: They . . . we don't have no power. I was so alone
after you left. Was I alone in the world by myself. And
everybody going about their business as if nothing didn't
happen. As if we didn't march. As if we didn't shout. As if
. . . as if nutten. And then I had to ask myself, what it is
you believe in, Marva? What it is you believing in? Where
your life going? Sometimes is only the Bible. Cause is hard
for one person by herself to believe alone. You have to
believe in a company, with other people. So . . .

ROOSO: So?

CALLISTE: So what I really saying is that I don't want to be a
traitor again. Is best I just live like everybody else.

ROOSO: Not believing in nothing? Just going so? I sorry is so
you see things. [CALLISTE *is pensive*. ROOSO *speaks
sympathetically*] What about the child?

CALLISTE: She's okay.

ROOSO: When you alone, you have to begin alone. You have to
begin to believe alone. That is something we have to learn.

CALLISTE: If you have the strength.

PRIME [*urgently, pleading, to* CALLISTE]: But, he's alive. He's alive
again. You are not no where again. You are not alone
again.

ABLACK [*sharply*]: Miss Prime!

PRIME [*hesitates*]: Yes, sir.

ABLACK: Do not be amazed. Periodically we have such
performances here. Conscience, defeat, frustration; people
seeking to reclaim what they never worked for, making
grand speeches that mock their powerlessness. You belong
to none of this. It doesn't concern you. Here you have an
opportunity to get ahead, to capitalize on your education
and training and rise above your brethren.

ROOSO [*assertively*]: I am alive! [*he begins to unbotton his trousers,*

takes them off] Here is the other part of your costume, Mr
Ablack.

ABLACK: Hear! hear! hear! [*applauding in a mocking way*] So you
do it? You let craziness prevail. Hear, hear, hear. Well, at
least, let's be glad that jockey shorts is not part of the issue
of uniform, otherwise patient as I am, I would have had to
alert the police about indecent exposure.

ROOSO [*to audience*]: Yes, applaud now, for this is my last
performance, my last role. The world is really not a stage,
you know. Sometimes you get ketch. You forced to play a
part that is not yourself. I play slave, guerrilla. I follow the
crowd, play marcher, play servant, savage, skylarker,
security, announcer, bad john, chuckouter. And I . . . I is
really just a man who fighting to begin his living. I ain't no
real terror, you know. I love people. I love this island. But I
ain't stupid. Sometimes I does wonder what make people
think that I, of all, must give up the right to my life. I say is,
because I does look too ordinary. Maybe my face stupidee.

ABLACK [*interrupting*]: You sure this is not a role too, this one?
You not playing this one for me?

ROOSO [*a sternness, almost a rigidity, comes over him*]: No, my
Brother. I could play a role in front strangers, in front
people who don't know me; but, you. You damn fool! You
damn fool! You don't know that roles finish playing
between you and me. You don't understand that I can't go
through with you what I go through with Cherry. I cry A
A Ah Black too! How I could play a role in front of you?

ABLACK [*groping for an accusation*]: That's the difference between
me and Cherry. I too familiar with you. From Cherry you
accept success, but not from me, never from me. We must
be together on the same scale forever at the bottom of the
ladder: old nigger! Proletariat! Scrunter!

ROOSO: Success? You successful? Look, Ablack, don't play that
role with yourself. Don't do it. [*He softens*] Look, man, we
come in town together, you and me. Young, proud, strong.
And we watch the scenery, and without nobody telling us
nothing, we did know, Ashton, that is not so things should
be. We did know that we was more than beast, that our

struggle was to become human, to become holy. We was
people, Ashton. What make you feel that you have to give
that up?

ABLACK: So you retire? You ready now to go in the hills and full
up your head with ganja?

ROOSO: Retire? Me? Is you who retire, brother. Listen, I come
in town young, strong, full with my rhythm. I play The
Glory of Greece, The Fall of Babylon. I stand my hand like
a man. My headpiece is still this island. I have no wheels
to ease the strain, I have no wings to fly. What happen?
You think because I dancing I don't feel the weight,
holding it up here alone?

ABLACK: You like it so.

ROOSO: I know that I is the one that bend the wire. I know I is
the song composer; but I can't carry it alone for ever.

PRIME: Mr Rooso! Mr Rooso!

ROOSO: Many times I does feel to let it go, let it fall, just to see
what will happen. But I holding it up so long. Though I is
not the owner, I feel like it is my one alone . . . Maybe you
right, you know. I ain't have nothing . . . All I have to
show is this island crown, this shining headpiece that
pressing me down. Nobody want it on their shoulder.
They want wings, wheels, something easy, balloons,
maybe. Imagine, balloons to hold up a headpiece. We
forgetting the art of responsibility, leaving the hard work
to the next person while we have a good time . . . a good
time. Everybody want to jump up in the band, for the
world to see them out in front waving the flag, and leave it
to others to always beat the pan. That is why some days
you hardly have any music: the panman want a little time
to dance with his woman . . . People have to change in this
country. We have to pull up we socks. Cause we have
children coming. Nice nice children. I can't tell who is
their father, which is yours and which is mine, they all
resemble so much. I ain't have nothing to give them except
the promise of these islands and to show them how to hold
up the headpiece, how to balance it when the strong wind
blowing, how to move and take the pressure; and when

they parading, how to dance it strong, to show off the colours how they harmonise so that the whole grand stand of the world will see it shining like . . . like a star, a moon, a sun. But I . . . I is a dreamer . . . [*turning away*] I is a dreamer.

PRIME [*respectfully*]: Mr Rooso, I want to say I sorry.

ROOSO [*tenderly*]: Is all right, girl. Is all right.

ABLACK [*sternly*]: Miss Prime, this does not concern you!

ROOSO [*To* PRIME]: I know you had something in you. I see you come in this store, with stupidness plaster all over you face, making you stiff. And behind it, I see your beauty. And I don't know how to talk to you, how to make you know that you is the promise and to not throw yourself away.

PRIME: Now I understand daddy.

ROOSO: Cause you is the inspiration that make the promise fresh again and give me strength again so I could go again and know it have a reason for me to bear the strain.

PRIME *nods with understanding*.

ABLACK: Miss Prime, what is wrong with you? You are an intelligent girl. You have your 'A' levels. This doesn't concern you, the past, Cherry, slavery. You grow up on junior sec, senior sec, secretarial schools. You not from the University of Woodford Square.

CALLISTE *is looking at* ROOSO *with new understanding*.

ROOSO: So, goodbye. All of you, goodbye. [*to* CALLISTE] And that song, that song to you? Well, I think I have it now. It clear to me. [*he sings*]
> The same song for you
> Is the same song for she
> The song I sing for you
> Is my song for everybody
> My love for you

        Is the same love for she
        I don't love you less
        Cause I love everybody
        You disappointed?

CALLISTE: Well . . . It surprise me, I mean, yes. I did expect
    something special.

PRIME [*singing*]:
        The same love for you
        Is the same love for you
        Can I love her less
        When I love you so sincerely

ROOSO: You know, I was really trying to sing a special song for
    you, something for you alone to lift you up, after all the
    pressure you undergo. Queen of African beauty, my black
    lovey dovey; but I find in you I does see everybody, and
    when I look at other people you there too. You
    understand?

CALLISTE: Thank you, thank you.

PRIME *goes up to him. He stretches out his hand, she stretches out hers.
They shake hands.* PRIME *draws away then leans over and kisses him on
the cheek.* ROOSO *turns to exit.* CALLISTE *takes up her handbag.*

ABLACK [*to* CALLISTE]: You going too?
CALLISTE: I ain't take lunch yet, Mr Ablack.

ROOSO *is moving off.*

ABLACK: So, Rooso, what you going to do for a living?
ROOSO: Live, Mr Ablack. Live.
ABLACK: Lovely! [*With controlled fury that eventually breaks out*]
    But, remember, when Ash Wednesday come and pass and
    everybody go back to their race and to their class, don't
    put your arse in front this door. Just make sure that you
    get people to change the world with you. Go on.
CALLISTE: We have to believe, Mr Ablack.
ABLACK [*emphatically*]: The world is what it is. It is not a dream.
ROOSO: The world is what we make it.

PRIME [*excitedly*]: And we keep on making it what we would like it to be, by what we do.

ROOSO: By our will.

ABLACK [*interrupting, authoritatively*]: Listen, man. I telling you . . .

CALLISTE: Let him talk, Mr Ablack. You always cutting him off, ridiculing him, reducing him to a joke whatever he saying. And by what authority? We live life too, we feel too. We think too.

ABLACK [*laughing*]: Ha! Ha ha! Romeo and Juliet, Suzie and Sambo. I was just going to remind you that this is just an island. We only part of something that they directing from another region. You could change that?

PRIME: That's not fair. You changing the subject.

ABLACK: Young lady, this is not a classroom discussion. This is the world. This, as Suzie and Sambo would say, is life.

ROOSO: You see all this talk to stop me living, don't worry with me. You see me, I have a life that I battle for to live and I going to live it. I not alone in the world. I don't have the answer to every question. I is just a beginning, a part, a step. People coming. Children coming, from San Juan and Nelson Street, from Chaguanas, Flanagin Town, Cascade, Laventille. They streaming down from the hills, they rising out of the junior secs and senior comprehensive, real children seeking a life, looking for a world to live in . . . Lord, I hope them people still waiting.

ROOSO *exits quickly.* CALLISTE *follows.* PRIME *takes up her handbag.* ABLACK *looks on sullenly as his staff leave.*

PRIME [*to* ABLACK]: Mr Ablack, maybe you should come and hear him. It might make you feel better.

ABLACK: Just see that you get back here on time.

PRIME *exits. Alone,* ABLACK *paces the length of the store.*

ABLACK [*with forced laughter*]: Ha! ha! The arse. The same love for you is the same love for she. Nice. Nice . . . [*he*

contemplates his situation] I going to make a new rule: Lunch
hour not to be used for listening to calypso. No. [*he smiles
wickedly*] I'll change the lunch hour to 11.00. He does sing
at 12.00. SPITEFUL BITCH! Can't stand to stay and see
me succeed. Can't stand my success! I will get new people.
Young people. Boys from trade schools, girls with
secretarial certificates. New people who don't bear me no
grudge, who don't know Cherry, who don't feel I owe
them nothing. Workers who could calculate like machines.
[*he hears the sound of a truck*] Ah! At last the truck with the
wrought iron reach. Let me go and get Sam to offload it [*he
goes to the door leading to the back of the store*] Sam! Sam! [*heavy
rockers music – Bob Marley's 'We Have a Life to Live'*] Sam,
turn off that blasted music! The truck with the wrought
iron reach. What? You ain't finish stack up the plywood
yet? What? . . . Sam, well I have to shout at I-man [*pause*] I
say you holding up my work. [*under his breath*] Well, what
the arse is this? [*he moves from the door, goes wearily to the chair
vacated by* CALLISTE. *He is about to sit*] I suppose he is the next
one I have to deal with now. [*music rises*] I suppose so, yes.

Music fills the theatre, lights fade.

   CURTAIN

My Name is Village

Play in Two Acts

Dedicated to Lena Henry, Irvine Fortune, Una
Homeward and Matura Villagers

My Name is Village was first performed by the Matura Villagers
at Queen's Hall, Port of Spain in September 1976 with the
following cast:

CYRIL VILLAGE, Irvine Fortune
MISS EVVIE, Gloria Lewis
ROY, Franklyn Henry
QUICKLEY, Tony Hernandez
SMART, Clarence Guevera
BLOCKO, Selwyn Homeward
SONNY, Nowill Hector
SCRATCH, Trevor Villafana
WESTERN, Ruthven Alcindor
TOWN TEST, Ramesh Singh
YES MEN, Glen Elder and Stephen Matthew
ELENA, Debbie Anthony
BETTY, Isidora Fortune
MISS STUCK UP, Lena Henry
ANGELINA, Brenda Augustine
REBECCA, Sharon Anthony
MARKET WOMEN, Una Homeward, Eutrice Augustine and
    Pearline Findlay
BOY, Glen Hector
GIRL, Lorna Charles
SCHOOLGIRLS, Sharon Anthony, Judith Anthony,
    Stephanie Guevera and Gwendolyn Matthew
POLICEMAN, Cecil Mitchell
Directed by Earl Lovelace
Choreographer, Lena Henry

Characters

CYRIL VILLAGE
MISS EVVIE, his wife
ROY, his son
QUICKLY
SMART } Roy's friends
BLOCKO
SONNY, an ageing quatro player
SCRATCH, a drunkard
WESTERN, a nightwatchman
TOWN TEST, exponent of progress
His two YES MEN
ELENA, a highschool girl
BETTY, her friend
MISS STUCK UP
ANGELINA, Elena's mother
A Constable
A Market Sweeper
Various schoolgirls and schoolboys
Various market women
Various other villagers

Act One

Scene One

Evening. Villagers going home from the field, bearing the tools of their labour. The villagers sing a work song, one not so much of celebration as of survival, telling of an inner strength and resilience ('Weigh weigh weigh the man down, weigh the man down, weigh the man down). *Four young men stand sullenly on the corner and watch them. Then as the villagers go off they begin karate exercises. Karate movements become a dance punctuating the village song. It is a dance telling of their frustration, their strength and quickness, and not knowing what to do with themselves. The fellows continue dancing.* ROY *begins to sing* (backed by the choir).

> What's my thing
> Who am I
> Where am I going
> Where am I going
> What is my future
> What's my fight
> I'm so young
> Is it night
> Is it night

> CHORUS: Weigh weigh weigh the man down
> weigh the man down, weigh the man down.

> What's my thing
> Who am I
> What is my future
> What is my fight
> What am I doing
> With all my might
> It's too early
> For it to be night

CHORUS: Weigh, weigh [*repeat as above*]

The young men position themselves on stage as the girls enter doing their own graceful dance. ROY *continues singing as long as the girls dance on stage. As the girls exit the singing stops.*

QUICKLEY: I wish them fellars was still on the hills, I woulda go and join them.

SMART: Which fellars?

QUICKLEY: Them guerrillas and them. [*earnestly*] Them fellars had something to fight for.

BLOCKO: Them was real crazy fellars, eh!

ROY: What they was fighting for?

BLOCKO: I don't know man, I know they was fighting.

QUICKLEY: Yes, they was fighting [*as if he wished he was with them*].

ROY: Yes, they was fighting [*understanding dawning upon him*].

SMART: Yeah, them fellars was fighting.

ROY: I wish *I had something* to fight *for*. Like a war.

BLOCKO [*admiringly*]: Them was real crazy fellers; them guerrillas.

Enter ELENA *a highschool girl on her way home. Behind her are her school friends.*

QUICKLY [*to* ROY]: Hey man! Look who passing! You want me to call she for you!

ROY *looks around confused.*

SMART [*to* ROY]: Ain't you like the girl.

QUICKLY: I feel she like you too.

SMART: Pssssssst.

BLOCKO: Hey, Miss, Roy want to talk to you.

ELENA *moves self consciously.* ROY *hesitates. Walks towards her.*

ROY [*to* BLOCKO]: Hey, don't heckle that girl, boy. [*softly*

to ELENA] Elena! [ELENA *comes to a stop. She doesn't answer*]
Elena! I like you, you know.

ELENA: Well, don't worry to like me.

ROY: But I like you.

School girls come up from behind.

ELENA [*to* ROY]: You ain't tired heckle me?

GIRLS: Yes everytime she pass you heckling she. [*they giggle
      loudly*]

ROY: I ain't heckling she. I like she. [*looking at* ELENA *softly*]

GIRLS: Yes, you heckling she. [*they laugh again*]

Boys start singing and girls join in.

> Everytime she pass you heckling she
> Everytime she pass you heckling she
> I go tell she Mama don't send she down dey
> I go tell she Mama don't send she down dey
>
> Everytime she pass you trouble she
> Everytime she pass you trouble she
> I go tell she Mama don't send she down dey
> I go tell she Mama don't send she down dey.
>
> Everytime she pass you whistle she
> Everytime she pass you whistle she
> I go tell she Mama don't send she down dey
> I go tell she Mama don't send she down dey.

As the singing continues ELENA's *mother* ANGELINA *enters in a huff and
speaks loudly. The singing stops.*

ANGELINA: YOU don't have to tell me nothing. I [*stressing*] see
      everything. [*she approaches* ROY *who backs away*] You see this
      girl, have nothing to tell her. We only here because we
      living here. What you want to do with her, you Mr Roy?
      Carry her in the garden to plant dasheen? I spending my

money to send her to highschool. I don't want none of all
you to come and confuse she brain because soon as she
pass she exams she go leave this place.

BLOCKO: She go leave this place?

The boys start singing

> As soon as she pass she exam, she go leave this place
> She go leave this place, she go leave this place

The girls take up the song too.

> As soon as she pass she exam she go leave this place
> She go leave this place, she go leave this place
> As soon as she pass she exam, she go leave this place
> She go leave this place she go leave this place, Roy,
> Nothing to do with you, nothing to do with you,
> Nothing to do with you cause she going away.
>
> As soon as she pass she exam she go take a bus, she go
> take a train, she go take a plane
> As soon as she pass she exam she go take a bus, she go
> take a train, she go take a plane, Roy
> Nothing to do with you nothing to do with you, nothing
> to do with you nothing to do with you, cause she going
> away.
>
> As soon as she pass she exam she go leave this place,
> she go leave this place she go leave this place,
> As soon as she pass she exam she go leave this place,
> she go leave this place, she go leave this place, Roy,
> Nothing to do with you, nothing to do with you,
> nothing to do with you cause she going away, she going
> away, she going away

The girls exit singing.

ROY [*thoughtfully, sadly: I wish them fellars was still on the hills, I woulda sure go and join them.*

Enter Town Test and two Yes Men.

TOWN TEST: Hello, Country Bookies, my name is Town Test.
YES MEN: Yes!
TOWN TEST: Ah selling dictionaries,
YES MEN: Dictionaries!
TOWN TEST: Encyclopedias,
YES MEN: Encyclopedias!
TOWN TEST: Bush rum and I taking up whe-whe marks. I have race programmes.
YES MEN: Race programmes!
TOWN TEST: Lottery.
YES MEN: Lottery!
TOWN TEST: The Bomb, and you could even get a little grass.
YES MEN: Yes!
TOWN TEST: These are my two yes men.
YES MEN: Yes.
TOWN TEST: I come to enlighten you, to make you hip, to get you with it.
YES MEN: Yes!
TOWN TEST: So I want everybody to say, YEAH! Say YEAH! Say YEAH!

YES MEN *and all the boys except* ROY *say* YEAH!

TOWN TEST [*going towards* ROY]: Wait! Who is you don't want to say Yeah! No. Don't tell me. Your name is Village. You is forest trees and manicou on a moonlight night. You is dirt road and crapaud singing in a shallow pond.
YES MEN [*making crapaud sounds*]: Pungala! . . . Pungala! . . .
TOWN TEST: You is cutlass and hoe tickling the earth, making grass laugh.
YES MEN [*laughing*]: Ha! ha! ha!

TOWN TEST: You is time behind time.

YES MEN: Time behind time.

TOWN TEST: You know the lady was right, what you could give daughter? You want to carry her to plant dasheen?

YES MEN: Dasheen? What is dasheen?

TOWN TEST: Man out there is a world of progress.

YES MEN: Progress.

TOWN TEST: Speed.

YES MEN: Speed.

TOWN TEST: Colour television.

YES MEN: Colour television.

TOWN TEST: Tall buildings.

YES MEN: Tall buildings.

TOWN TEST: Street lights.

YES MEN: Street lights.

TOWN TEST: Pool tables.

YES MEN: Pool tables.

TOWN TEST: Man you want to carry her to plant dasheen when you could be a sex machine.

YES MEN: Sex machine! Sex machine! Stay on the scene with a sex machine.

TOWN TEST: Man, this is a place just to grow you up.

YES MEN: To grow you up.

TOWN TEST: To tame you.

YES MEN: To tame you.

TOWN TEST: To domesticate you.

YES MEN: Domesticate you.

TOWN TEST: So when you go out in the world you will say 'excuse me'.

YES MEN: Excuse me, excuse me, excuse me.

TOWN TEST: You want to say excuse me, when you could say 'right on'.

YES MEN: Right on, brother.

TOWN TEST: You want to bow down when you could prance, you have to be a Jab Malassie in this world. Make them fraid you.

YES MEN: Fraid you.

TOWN TEST: Hit them low!

YES MEN : Hit them low!
TOWN TEST : Stamp them!
YES MEN : Stamp them!
TOWN TEST : Command them!
YES MEN : Command them!
TOWN TEST : Embarrass them.
YES MEN : Embarrass them!
TOWN TEST : Anything
YES MEN : Anything!
TOWN TEST : Anything . . .

TOWN TEST *turns around and sees a girl entering* — MISS STUCK UP.

TOWN TEST : Watch me! [*to girl*] Hey, come! [*commanding*]
STUCK UP [*hesitates*] : Who me, you calling?
TOWN TEST : Yes, Miss Pretty, you.

STUCK UP *comes forward hesitantly*.

TOWN TEST : Where you going so hurry, pretty girl?
STUCK UP : That ain't you business. [*she goes to move on, he blocks her path*]
TOWN TEST : Wait! Wait! That is my business. Any nice girl is my business. You know you nice?
STUCK UP [*stifles a smile*] : Mister, move outa my way, please.
TOWN TEST : You know you nice [*pause*] And you know something else? You like me.
STUCK UP : I . . . ?
TOWN TEST : YES! And you know why you like me? You fraid me. I make you tremble, not so?
STUCK UP : What you call me for?
TOWN TEST : I just call you to pinch you [*pinches her*] and to check you out.
STUCK UP [*coyly*] : You good yes.

TOWN TEST *puts his arm around her shoulders and they exit, followed by* YES MEN *who say a loud 'YES' in* ROY*'s ear. School boys enter laughing at* ROY *and his gang.*

ROY: Like to get them you have to command them!

QUICKLEY [*to school boys*]: Hey, all you, go on! Go on! Scram. Go
   from here. I say go.

ROY: No, leave them. Leave them. Let them learn. [*the school
   boys move forward*] To be a success in the world

BOYS: To be a success in the world

ROY: You have to be a Jab Malassie

BOYS: You have to be a Jab Malassie

ROY: Make them fraid you

BOYS: Make them fraid you

ROY: Hit them low

BOYS: Hit them low

ROY: Stamp them

BOYS: Stamp them

ROY: Command them.

BOYS: Command them.

ROY: Embarrass them.

BOYS: Embarrass them.

ROY: Anything, anything. [GIRL *enters stage,* ROY *turns
   and sees her*] Watch me! [*to girl*] Hey, come [*softly*] Hey,
   come! [*louder as she hesitates*]

The GIRL *turns.*

GIRL: Is me you calling?

ROY: Yes, Miss Pretty, you.

GIRL [*walking towards him wiggling her hips*]: And what you
   calling me for?

ROY: I just want to pinch you. [*pinches her*]

GIRL: That is all you call me for?

GIRL *laughs and makes as if she is going off stage.*

ROY [*loudly*]: Hey, come! Hey, come!

The GIRL *returns. Roy hugs her and they exit together.* ROY's *friends all
shout:* Hey, come! Hey, come! *The school boys go off stage and*

ROY's *friends are joined on stage by the girls. They all sing.*

> Hey come is you am calling
> What you playing
> Don't dig nothing
> I just want to pinch you
> And to check you out
> Keep outa trouble and out my mouth
> I don't want
> A girl like you
> To go astray, please stay.
>
> Hey come, is you am calling
> I ain't asking, I commanding
> I just want to pinch you
> And to hold you tight
> We young together, we don't have to fight.
> I don't want a girl like you
> To disappear, come here.
>
> Hey come is me they calling
> They ain't asking, they commanding
> I just want to pinch you
> And to hold you tight
> We young together, we don't have to fight
> I don't want a girl like you
> To disappear, come here.

A lively calypso dance is done by the girls and boys. They are happy and exuberant as if something in them has been unbottled.

Scene Two

The market place. The old women and the girls are buying and selling. The young men enter. The are noisy, rude and disruptive. They pull and tug at the girls. The girls scream. There is much confusion. The boys grab produce from the old women and they do not pay. One woman accosts one of the young men. He ignores her. She sets up an alarm.

FIRST WOMAN: He ain't pay! He ain't pay!

ANGELINA: [*to* MARKET SWEEPER]: Mister, you ain't see what going on. You ain't see how the boys take our goods and ain't pay? Do something.

SWEEPER: Lady, I just sweeping here, talk to the Constable!

ANGELINA: Constable, these boys take our goods and didn't pay. Do something please. Constable, you ain't see or what . . .

CONSTABLE *looks at his watch. He claps his hands. The place quietens.*

CONSTABLE: I off-duty.

The women all scream and rush after the CONSTABLE *who scampers off stage. The women and girls stay on stage. Jab Malassie drums are heard. Two Jab Malassies enter and do a Jab Malassie dance in which the girls are seduced. The old women look on at dance in amazement. The girls exit with the Jab Malassies. The market women start to sing.*

Aa! Aa! Aa! Aa!
Aa! Aa! Aa! Aa!

Is the times
Is the times
Is the times that come so
Is the times
Is the times
Is the times that come so
Is the times that come so

Is the times that come so
Is the times
Is the times
Is the times that come so

Aa! Aa! Aa! Aa!
Aa! Aa! Aa! Aa!

In rhythm with the song the women each speak in their turn:

FIRST WOMAN: Is how things twist and mix up. Like anything is everything, and everything is anything.

The other women repeat what she says. Then sing the chorus.

Is the times
Is the times
Is the times that come so

Aa! Aa! Aa! Aa!

ANGELINA: I say, is the men and them, they ain't like they used to be, they ain't have that sting, that weight, that authority.

Repeat and chorus.

Is the times
Is the times
Is the times that come so

Aa! Aa! Aa! Aa!

FIRST WOMAN: Is like they get tame, they get weary, lengay, like clothes that wring out.

The women sing the chorus.

Is the times
Is the times
Is the times that come so
Aa! Aa! Aa! Aa!

SECOND WOMAN: Maybe we fight them too much, oppose them
   much, doubt them too much.

The women repeat what she says and sing the chorus.

THIRD WOMAN: You know, I uses to admire the men and them
   so. I uses to sitdown and watch them walking, you know
   how they uses to walk, like the ground is they own and
   they chest is a wall and if they do their hands so [*stretching
   open her hands*] they part the world in two. I uses to watch
   them.
WOMEN: We used to watch them. (*They sing the chorus.*)
FIRST WOMAN: I uses to watch them and say. Oh! Lord, look
   how they walking, look how they strong! Look how they
   tall! Like they riding on horses.
OTHER WOMEN: Galloping, prancing.
THIRD WOMAN: And they going and they going, and with only
   two foot on the ground. I uses to watch them.
ANGELINA: Is like life beat them . . . Beat we too.
FIRST WOMAN: Is the liberation of this generation.
SECOND WOMAN: Is the change that come and lose we in it.
THIRD WOMAN: And a shame that come and bow we head, and
   we tongue get dumb and we voice can't raise.
ANGELINA: And no voice can't raise to say what is right and
   what wrong.
FIRST WOMAN: No. No, voice can't raise. For it ain't have no
   voice that have the right to raise.

All the women repeat what she says and sing the chorus.

ANGELINA: That is why I done tell Elena, as soon as she pass
   she exam she go leave this place.

Enter ELENA *and her friend* BETTY. ELENA *is crying.* BETTY *holds her comfortingly.*

ANGELINA [*alarmed*]: Elena! [*she rushes to* ELENA. *The other women gather around.*] Elena, what happen?

ELENA [*crying*]: Roy! Roy!

ANGELINA: Eh? What?

BETTY: Well, me and Elena was going down by the shop. Roy see she and say, 'Hey come!' and then she didn't go. So Roy come over by where she was walking and say, 'Hey, Girl, you ain't know I like you. [ELENA *cries harder*] and she say, 'Roy, ain't I tired tell you not to like me.'

ANGELINA: But look at the child's face how it bruise up. That boy feel because his name is Roy Village, he could do anything. Go on, let me hear what happen.

The women all crowd around to listen.

BETTY: And then Roy was walking by the canal. And Roy say, 'I could command you, you know. I could command you.' That is what he say. And Elena was walking by the canal too. And Roy say, 'If you don't want to come when I call you, I will push you down in the canal.' And she say, 'Roy, if you crazy push me down in the canal.' And he push she down in the canal. And she fall down in the canal.

ANGELINA: I going straight to the police! All you let me go.

The women try to restrain her.

FIRST WOMAN: Miss Angelina, don't get too hasty. Let us go and complain to the boy father [*leading* ANGELINA *to house*].

ANGELINA: Who Cyril? Cyril ain't know he head from his tail, I going to the police? Let me go.

FIRST WOMAN [*still restraining her*]: All right, well then, let's us go to the mother [*they walk*] look she right there on the gallery. [*they all stop in front of* MISS EVVIE'*s house*] Miss Evvie! Miss Evvie!

MISS EVVIE *stands on the veranda. A serious-looking woman.*

EVVIE: Morning, morning. What can I do for you.
ANGELINA [*angrily*]: Miss Evvie, I come to complain to you
    about your son.
EVVIE: Complain to me? What all you come to complain to me
    for? What happen?

They look at Betty.

BETTY: Well, me and Elena was going down by the shop. Roy
    see she and say, 'Hey come' and then she didn't come. So
    Roy come over by . . .
ANGELINA: Roy push this child down in the canal, and I going
    straight to the police.
FIRST WOMAN: Is a little trouble is so before police have to
    intervene I say is better we come and talk to you first.
EVVIE: Talk to me? What all you come to talk to me for? Put
    him in the police hands, put him in jail, because I tired. I
    tired. I ain't able. I ain't able [*as if on the verge of a
    breakdown*]. As for his father, all he could do is drink rum.
    Put him in jail. That is all the advice I could advise you.
    Put him in jail. What else could I say?

The crowd begins to chant . . . 'Put him in jail'.

    Put him in jail
    Put him in jail
    Put him in jail I say
    Put him in jail
    Put him in jail
    Ah don't care what nobody say
    Put him in jail
    Put him in jail I say
    Put him in jail
    Put him in jail
    Nobody to stand his bail

The women exit and the girls enter and do a dance to the tune of 'Put him in jail'. *They exit at the end of the dance.*

EVVIE [*as if the seriousness of the situation hits her*]: All you wait, wait. Somebody come please.

Enter BETTY

BETTY: Yes, Miss Evvie.
EVVIE: Betty, you know Mr Cyril, Roy father? Go and call him for me. Run, quick.
BETTY: But Miss Evvie, where I will find him this hour?
EVVIE: Look by Jaikoo or Mendoza. He must be in one of them rum shop.

BETTY *runs off.* EVVIE *walks worriedly into her house.*

Act Two

Scene One

It is evening. The scene is the culvert at the village corner. WESTERN, *a nightwatchman, waits for the bus.* SONNY, *an ageing man, plays the quatro. It is a nostalgic tune suggesting an earlier certainty and brightness, conjuring up market people going home in the evening, baskets on their heads. Enter* CYRIL VILLAGE *with a small parcel in his hand. He is a sensitive, combative fellow. He has had a few drinks and he comes along slowly. He stands, listening to* SONNY *play. The music captures him. He rests down his parcel and listens.*

CYRIL: You know you could play Sonny! [SONNY *smiles and continues.* CYRIL *centre stage*] You know how long I ain't hear a tune like that. Is like these tunes gone outa the village, gone outa life, gone outa the world. [*to* SONNY] Play it a little harder for me, let me dance.

SONNY *nods and plays on.* CYRIL *is about to dance. Enter* BETTY.

BETTY [*hurriedly, anxiously*]: Mr Cyril, Mr Cyril, Miss Evvie calling you.
CYRIL: Wait, let me hear the music and you go on home.
BETTY: But Mr Cyril, Miss Evvie calling you.
CYRIL [*irritated*]: I say WAIT and you go home. Play the music for me Sonny.
WESTERN [*teasing*]: Cyril, why you don't take the parcel and go home. You wife send you on a message, you want to dance. You getting mannish you know. What you have in the parcel there? [*he takes up the parcel and smells*] Saltfish? [*he begins to sing*] Saltfish, nothing in the world sweeter than saltfish.
CYRIL: Play that tune again, Sonny, [*to* WESTERN] and you put down my parcel.
WESTERN: You know that woman don't make joke. You remember the time she bust you head by the savannah!

You still have the cut? [*he makes to touch* CYRIL'*s head*] Let me
see. Why you don't take your parcel and go home? Like
you want another bust head or what?

CYRIL: No, I don't want another bust head. You right. You
right. Let me take me parcel and go home. [*he takes up his
parcel and makes as if to exit*]

WESTERN [*he moves towards* CYRIL. CYRIL *stops*]: You know you
vex. [*to* SONNY] You know he vex! Why you vex for? We is
we. We must make jokes. [*appeasing*] Look! Wait, Scratch
bringing a drink. Wait and take one.

CYRIL [*takes a step backwards from* WESTERN'*s reach*]: That is a
joke? That is joke?

Enter SCRATCH, *a drunkard don't-care-damn fellow. He has a bottle of
rum.*

WESTERN: Ah! Look Scratch reach with the rum. [*he takes bottle
and cup from* SCRATCH. *He takes a drink and pours one for* CYRIL
and hands it to him] Take a drink man, you wife only bust
you head, you know what mine do. [CYRIL *does not take the
drink. To* SCRATCH] You know, I make a joke with the man
and he vex.

SCRATCH [*to* CYRIL]: You vex, Cyril. You vex! If a man make a
joke, a man make a joke. What is a joke? If people didn't
make joke, what would happen. Everybody woulda be
fighting! [*chucking* CYRIL] You want to fight him? You want
to fight him? [*chucking* CYRIL *again.* CYRIL *stands stiffly,
seriously.* SCRATCH *offers him the bottle*] Take a drink! [CYRIL
still does not respond] You want to fight me? You want to
fight me?

CYRIL: I don't want to fight nobody.

SCRATCH: Well shut you damn mouth and take the drink.
[CYRIL *takes the drink.* SCRATCH *takes* CYRIL'*s parcel and flings it
on the ground. He puts his arm around* CYRIL'*s shoulder and begins
to dance as he sings: 'Is so we is in Trinidad, sweet sweet
Trinidad'.* CYRIL *pulls away*]

CYRIL: But I don't like how the man talk to me. [*thinking about
his dignity, growing irritated. To* WESTERN] I don't like how
the man talk to me. I don't like how you talk to me boy!

You shoulda never talk to me so. I don't like it.

WESTERN [*becoming serious*]: You get old Cyril. You can't even
  take a joke.

CYRIL: That is a joke? I name Cyril Village and a man have to
  know how to talk to me. [*striking chest and advancing on*
  WESTERN] I name Village and a man have to know how to
  talk to me.

SCRATCH: Who the hell is you Cyril? You stupid or what?
  People does say anything now. They does talk to anybody,
  anyhow.

CYRIL: In my days boy, in my day when I was Village and a
  man talk to me so [*looking up and holding his head*] oh, Lord!
  Oh, Lord!

SCRATCH: [*deliberately*]: In your days, my arse. In your days my
  arse. [*with emphasis*] In your days . . . [*he pauses and
  remembers, touches his collar as if fixing tie*] I was a
  schoolteacher. Today ain't nobody day. It ain't nobody
  day.

WESTERN: You get old Cyril. Your wife busting your head, your
  children ruling you and you just walking around with two
  drinks in your head, waiting for somebody to sorry for you.
  Well, I sorry for you. Better take your parcel and go home.

CYRIL [*challenged and striking chest and approaching*
  WESTERN]: My name is Village. I name Village!

SONNY: Come out from there Cyril! Come out from there boy!

CYRIL: I was a lion in this place. Not a stickman to stand up to
  me. I go Grande and fight Prengay. You forget me Boy!
  You forget my name!

CYRIL *goes into stighfight stance and starts to dance and sing. Choir
backstage takes up chant.*

  Hurray! hurrah
  Hurray! hurrah this morning
  Hurray! hurrah
  Hurray! hurrah this morning
  Hurray! hurrah bois man dead for Village coming
  Hurray! hurrah

CYRIL, *still in stickfight stance, challenges* WESTERN *who is reluctant to accept.* CYRIL *persists and* WESTERN *cuffs him down.* WESTERN *and* SCRATCH *exit. While* CYRIL *is on the ground three stickmen do a kalinda dance reminiscent of* CYRIL *when he was champion. The chant continues during the dance. Stickmen exit.* SONNY *goes to* CYRIL *and shakes him.*

SONNY: You okay, man? You okay?

CYRIL *sits up.*

CYRIL: What happen to life Sonny? [*puts his cap on and stands up*]
SONNY: Is old we get Cyril. We get old.
CYRIL: I had no right to get vex. I don't know what madness come in my head.
SONNY: Is old we get Cyril. We get old and this place ain't ours again. But you put up a good fight Cyril. You give him a good blow.
CYRIL: And he knock me down. And my face swell up.
SONNY: But you get up, you stand up, you walking Cyril.
CYRIL: We get too old to fight Sonny. We get too old.
SONNY: How we get too old Cyril? How a man could get too old? Eh, Hombre? How you could get too old? [*chucking him in a friendly, masculine way*] I tell you you give him a good blow.
CYRIL [*smiling in agreement*]: Yes, I give him a good blow. [*becoming boastful*] And you know Sonny, I coulda mash up his tail for him. I coulda beat that man like a snake if I had my poui.
SONNY: Yes Cyril. You still have the power in you.
CYRIL: You right you know, Sonny. A man can't get too old to fight. A man could never get too old to fight.

CYRIL *and* SONNY *start to sing.*

> A man can't get too old to fight
> A man can't get too old to fight
> When fight come he have to fight
> If he is a man

When fight come he have to fight
San humanite

A man can't get too old to dream
A man can't get too old to dream
When dream come he have to dream
When he is a man
When dream come he have to dream
San humanite

A man can't be afraid to fall
A man can't be afraid to fall
The best of man does take a fall
When he is a man
The best a man does take a fall
Is the better man does rise again.

A man can't get too old to fight
A man can't get too old to fight
When fight come he have to fight
When he is a man
When fight come he have to fight
San humanite.

Scene Two

CYRIL's *yard. He enters with his new dignity.* EVVIE, *his wife, sits puffed up in the verandah waiting.*

CYRIL [*loud*]: Evvie! [*louder*] Evvie!

EVVIE *approaches him, her hand outstretched for the parcel. He hands it to her.*

EVVIE [*coldly*]: Thank you! Thank you! [*calling*] Rebecca,
    Rebecca, put this in the pot.

Enter REBECCA

REBECCA [*looking at the parcel*]: Saltfish mammy?

EVVIE: Yes. [REBECCA *takes parcel and exits. To* CYRIL] I just want
    to tell you Cyril, I ain't able. You hear Cyril, I ain't able.
    The children getting big, the house ain't build, and
    Caroline ain't reach from school yet.

CYRIL: I was coming home long time you know, but . . .

EVVIE: But what? The rum was too sweet, and your friends was
    too precious. [CYRIL *smiles*] And you smiling? What so
    funny for you to smile at?

CYRIL: I watching how your mouth moving smooth, smooth,
    smooth! Fast, fast, fast! How all these years I coming
    home, you never ask me no question. What happen to me
    or anything?

EVVIE: What question you want me to ask you?

CYRIL: But I have something to tell you. I have something to
    tell you.

EVVIE [*seeing* CYRIL*'s face draws nearer to* CYRIL *to examine his face*]:
    What happen to your face?

CYRIL [*boastfully*]: I was in a fight today.

EVVIE: You gone back fighting again? [*disbelief*] I thought you
    did finish with that long ago? I really see you face but I say
    you get drunk and fall down in a canal. I didn't know you
    was in a fight. I really thought you did finish with that?

CYRIL: Well! I fighting again! [*striking his chest*] Village fighting
    again! Hear this, all you inside this house, Village fighting
    again and from today . . . all shit cut out. I fighting again!

EVVIE: You too late Cyril. You too late to come here smiling
    and shout out 'you fighting again'. You should be fighting
    to build the house and keep your children straight. You
    should be fighting to give Roy something to hold on to.
    Not leaving him to be a Jab Malassie. Frightening people
    children and making me shame. You know what happen

today? A whole band of people come and complain here
about how Roy misbehaving. But police will hold him.
You better do something. You have to do something Cyril!

CYRIL [*angrily*]: Where Roy? Where Roy? [CYRIL *rushes inside
the house*.]

REBECCA: He gone down by Mr Patrick wake.

CYRIL *grabs his stick and rushes out again*. EVVIE *grabs him*.

EVVIE: You can't go so Cyril. You can't go so. You can't go
with only your fighting. You have to try something more.

CYRIL: YOU have to try something too Evvie.

EVVIE: But what I could try? I talk to the children, but they
wouldn't listen to me. I can't force them.

CYRIL: But you have to give something . . . we have to give
something! But what?

CYRIL *moves away from her and starts to sing. All the children join him
on stage and the children sing the chorus*

> What can we give when there's nothing to give
> And we've lost our authority
> Can't understand the children
> What can we give to them.

CHORUS: We are the plants
> Waiting for the dew drops of your caring
> We are your children
> Waiting for the hand of your love
> Give love, give love, give love
> Give love, give love, give love

> What can we sing when we've sung every song
> And they don't like the tune
> We can't control the children
> What can we sing to them

CHORUS: We are the trees

> Waiting for the breeze of your caring
> We are the seas
> Waiting for the rivers of your love
> Sing love, sing love, sing love.
>
> What can we do
> When we've done everything
> And they keep going astray
> We can't control the children
> What's there to do again

CHORUS: We are the plants
> Waiting for the dewdrops of your caring
> We are your children
> Waiting for the hand of your love
> Give love, give love, give love
> Give love, Give love, give love
> Give love, give love, give love
> Give love, give love, give love

Children exit. CYRIL *moves to leave too.*

EVVIE: Cyril, look I was just prettying up the house and as you going to see Roy to carry this for him. [*hands* CYRIL *a little bouquet of flowers*].

Scene Three

Patrick's wake. The villagers at the wake sing hymns, dance bongo, play games. ROY *is beating two sticks together and is in the middle of a disorderly group comprising his friends.* CYRIL *enters from stage left. He walks around peeping here and there trying to locate* ROY. *After a while he sees* ROY. *He stands and watches him. The bongo tune is uppermost at the time. It drowns out everything else. Roy leads the singing:*

Archie Boule Boule, Archie Boule
Oy Oy Oy, Archie Boule
My mother send me to school, Archie Boule.
My teacher call me a fool, Archie Boule
My teacher tell me to wine,
And I wine like a bail of twine.

CYRIL *still stands looking at* ROY. *He hits stick on bench. The song stops.*

CYRIL [*to* ROY]: Boy, I want to talk to you. ROY *comes towards him and they move down centre stage*] I want to talk to you. But I don't know what to tell you.

ROY: Pa, I don't know if you could tell me anything, you know.

CYRIL: Why I can't tell you anything. You interfering with people children. You going about life like a Jab Malassie, trying to dirty everybody. Why I can't tell you anything?

ROY: Pa, we had this kinda talk already. Tell me something new.

CYRIL: What to tell you?

ROY: Tell me how to be a winner. Tell me how to be a man. I don't want to play dolly house with my life. I don't want to go around bending my head saying 'Excuse me!' I want to be a man.

CYRIL: Your name is Village, Roy.

ROY: And because my name is Village, I must be a nobody. I want to be somebody. I don't want to end up like no old stickman like you with so much bust head that I frighten to fight.

CYRIL: Boy, the world is still the world, life is still life and people is still people. And when you play a Jab Malassie with your life you dirty yourself too.

ROY: Everybody doing it Pa. Big, big men that you look up to. Them too is Jab Malassie.

CYRIL: You dirty yourself boy!

ROY: Maybe that is what wrong with you, Pa. You don't want to get dirty. You want to through the world meek and mild and innocent as a baby. I is a man, Pa.

CYRIL: Your name is Village. And you is more than a Jab
      Malassie.

ROY: I want to be big, I want people to see me, to know my
      name. I want to be hip. Style. I want when you open the
      Bomb you see me on the scene. I want to be big!

CYRIL [*pauses and thinks*]: Maybe you right. I don't want to get
      dirty. Maybe I don't have enough greatness in me, enough
      chief, enough king, but today I was in a fight and a man
      cuff me down.

ROY [*concerned*]: Who cuff you, Pa?

CYRIL: Don't worry with who cuff me. A man cuff me down
      and I get up. [ROY *looks at him with some respect*] I fighting.
      And you say I is a old stickman with only bust head. And
      look at you! You quick! Look at your speed! You faster
      than Joe Louis. You is the new times. Kung Fu.
      Mohammed Ali. You want to be a Jab Malassie?

ROY: I want to be big!

CYRIL: I like the word you say. I want to be big. I like it. Boy,
      this world is we world because is we who love it and with
      we hands make things grow out of it. Is we own boy. And
      all them big devils of the world, who walking on we
      because they think is theirs alone, if you join them, you'll
      have to fight me. You'll have to fight me. Look your
      mother send this for you. [*hands* ROY *the flowers*]

The crowd at the wake starts to sing

      Jesus is a main line
      Tell him what you want
      Tell him what you want
      Tell him what you want
      Jesus is a main line
      Tell him what you want
      Tell him what you want right now.

      If you want pardon
      If you want peace
      If you want pardon

Bow down on Jesus knees

Sign my name, sign my name up there
Sign my name, sign my name up there

Touch my finger with a golden pen
A golden pen
A golden pen
Touch my finger with a golden pen
Sign my name there.
Sign my name
Sign my name up there

Enter TOWN TEST *followed by* YES MEN *and converts. The singing stops.*

TOWN TEST [*to* ROY]: Hello Country Man!
ROY: Hello Town Man!

Enter CONSTABLE, ANGELINA *and* ELENA. CYRIL *and* ANGELINA *mime a discussion.*

CONSTABLE: Who name Roy Village here?
ROY: I name Roy Village.
TOWN TEST [*with authority*]: Constable! I am speaking to this
     man!
CONSTABLE: Excuse me! Excuse me! [*he withdraws respectfully*]
TOWN TEST: [*to ROY*] You ready to go. You see all these fellars,
     all of them going with me [*he makes a sweeping motion with his
     hand over his followers*]. If you having any problems tell me.
     You know [*he puts his hand in his fob as if to withdraw money*].
     A man like you could be real big in town. Real Big. Any
     kind a contact, I have it. You coming? [ROY *shakes his head*]
     You is a real country bookie! So we draw swords eh!
     [*lifting his stick*] We is enemy. [*he starts to leave*]
ROY: We go meet Mr Jab Malassie.
YES MEN: Right on, brother!

Exit TOWN TEST *and his followers.* CYRIL *and* ANGELINA *still miming a discussion.* ROY *moves towards* ELENA.

ROY [*to* ELENA]: You get a hard fall?

ELENA: You push me down and you asking me if I get a hard fall!

ROY: I sorry! I sorry for true. Look I bring these flowers for you. ELENA *takes the flowers and softens towards* ROY. *She looks at him*] A man is flowers too and I sorry . . . and if you could be my friend.

ELENA: When I pass my exam I still going away.

ROY: But you still here and I still here. This is where we is now, for this world is we world girl, for us to care in and fight for. For all of us going away from here one time or the other. [*he continues*] You going to be my friend?

Holding hands the girls make a circle around them, and they start to dance and sing.

> See see moriah? moriah? moriah
> See see moriah, moriah, moriah
> Camboolay, lay, lay, lay, lay, ooo
> Camboolay
> See see moriah, moriah, moriah
> See see moriah, moriah, moriah.

While the singing is going on EVVIE *enters. She is surprised.*

EVVIE: Cyril, what happening here? Look at the children how beautiful they is.

CYRIL: But Evvie, we is people, we is people.

Lights slowly brighten and everybody starts to sing the village song.

> I am the earth
> I am the grass
> I am the village
> In which I live
> Where people plant
> And live as one

Unity forever is going on

From dust to dawn
And all day long
In which I toil
Digging the soil
Bamboos tall and evergreen
Living people and not machines

I am the earth
I am the grass
I am the village
In which I live
I'm not a weekend
You come to spend
I am the village
Where people live.

CURTAIN